Gendering Modernism

Gendering Modernism

A Historical Reappraisal of the Canon

MARIA BUCUR

Bloomsbury Academic
An imprint of Bloomsbury Publishing Plc

B L O O M S B U R Y
LONDON · OXFORD · NEW YORK · NEW DELHI · SYDNEY

Bloomsbury Academic

An imprint of Bloomsbury Publishing Plc

50 Bedford Square	1385 Broadway
London	New York
WC1B 3DP	NY 10018
UK	USA

www.bloomsbury.com

BLOOMSBURY and the Diana logo are trademarks of Bloomsbury Publishing Plc

First published 2017

British Library Cataloguing-in-Publication Data
A catalogue record for this book is available from the British Library.

ISBN: HB: 978-1-3500-2624-7
PB: 978-1-3500-2625-4
ePDF: 978-1-3500-2623-0
eBook: 978-1-3500-2626-1

Library of Congress Cataloging-in-Publication Data
Names: Bucur-Deckard, Maria, 1968- author.
Title: Gendering modernism: a historical reappraisal of the canon / Maria Bucur.
Description: London; New York: Bloomsbury Academic, an imprint of Bloomsbury Publishing
Plc, 2017. | Includes bibliographical references and index. Identifiers: LCCN 2016051242 | ISBN
9781350026247 (hardback) | ISBN 9781350026254 (paperback) | ISBN 9781350026230 (PDF) |
ISBN 9781350026261 (ePub) Subjects: LCSH: Women and the arts–United States–History–20th
century. | Women and the arts–Europe–History–20th century. | Arts, Modern–20th century. | Arts,
Modern–Philosophy. | Sex role–History–20th century. | Social movements–History–20th century. |
Arts and society–History–20th century. | United States–Intellectual life–20th century | Europe–
Intellectual life–20th century | BISAC: HISTORY / Modern / 20th Century. | HISTORY /
Social History. | SOCIAL SCIENCE / Gender Studies. Classification: LCC NX164.W65 B83 2017 |
DDC 700/.4522–dc23 LC record available at https://lccn.loc.gov/2016051242

Cover design by Adriana Brioso.
Cover image: *The Virgin*, 1913, by Gustav Klimt (1862-1918), oil on canvas. Prague,
Národní Galeri V Praze (National Fine Arts Museum) (© DeAgostini/Getty Images)

Typeset by Deanta Global Publishing Services, Chennai, India

To find out more about our authors and books visit www.bloomsbury.com.
Here you will find extracts, author interviews, details of forthcoming events
and the option to sign up for our newsletters.

Contents

List of Illustrations

Acknowledgments

This project came out of a wonderful lunch hosted by Marius Turda and Roger Griffin in Oxford, almost a decade ago. At that time, I was completing a book about war and memory and gave a talk on the gendered aspects of the construction of postwar memory in the 1920s in Romania. The book has undergone some transformations since then, but I am grateful to both of my hosts for encouraging me to begin and eventually finish it. As with any intellectual work I have done, the support of my family has been crucial to being able to follow my passions and still remain grounded. My husband Dan and sons, Dylan and Elvin, are the rock of my existence. This book would not have been possible without their help, love, and patience. Finally, my BYOB circle, my feminist fellow travelers have kept me going through many moments of self-doubt, exhaustion, and frustration. From Kristen to Krassi, from Mihaela to Melissa, from Marissa to Beth, I have drawn sustenance from their intellectual generosity, sense of humor, grit, and warmth. One of these great friends, who provided support and many delicious apple pies, passed away before the completion of this project. This book is dedicated to the memory of Katharine Jeffers, a bright light I miss every day.

Bloomington, October 2016

Prologue

A recent walk through Brussels reminded me of the continuing masculinist discursive force field in the European capitals that celebrate their modernist movements through public memorials, museums, art galleries, and sculpture gardens. Everywhere the visitor turns, plaques, sculptures, posters, postcards, and large billboards remind one of the art nouveau, symbolist, and surrealist great aesthetic revolts that started in the 1890s against the academic styles, bourgeois status quo, and comfortable self-important mediocrity of the 1880s. Among the star-studded panoply of Belgian modernists, René Magritte occupies an iconic place, reaffirmed in 2009 through the opening of a separate Magritte Museum next to the Musée de Beaux Arts.[1] Surreal windows painted as a blue sky with puffy white clouds adorned the façade of the Magritte Museum, branding it for all passersby as a Magritte artifact. What is not apparent until one visits the museum is the unquestioned canonic dominance of a vision of the modern crisis and modernist responses that cast men exclusively in the role of creator and women in the role of muse at best, and object of use, manipulation, conquest, and ridicule at worst. The museum's permanent exhibit never reflects on this recurrent aspect of Magritte's work, even as it exhibits sexually explicit pieces such as *Rape*, and sells postcards of works such as *The Eternal Evidence*.[2] This is something I want to take as a starting point for the goal of this book.

How is one to interpret the preponderance of subjects that deal with gender identity, gender relations, and the erotic in modernist cultural products, from literature to the visual arts, if not as evidence that gender norms were central to expressing anxieties and hopes for the aesthetic vision they were trying to articulate? Magritte used the naked body of his wife, Georgette, as the most frequent human subject of his art. What does that say about his aesthetic articulation of rejecting the past, God, family, and all the bourgeois facets of his upbringing, as he claimed to do early in life: "My art is only valid insofar as it resists bourgeois ideology, in the name of which life is extinguished."[3] And what does it mean for Magritte to offer the portrait of an indeterminate (though likely also based on Georgette) naked woman as the visual centerpiece of a 1929 survey taken by over a dozen modernist male artists and writers (see Figure 4, p. 41)?[4] When scholars and curators display such work as evidence of genius, creativity, and overall historical significance without any comment on the sexist language embedded in this vision, they are simply allowing new generations of viewers and readers to view the canon without any critical reflection about the misogyny of these artifacts.

We have Virginia Woolf on many reading lists for college literature courses, and Hannah Höch has made it into both important Dada exhibits and even textbooks. Still, the critiques of gender norms they and many other prominent artists, thinkers, and activists brought to modernism remain unevenly represented in the canon. We have over four decades of continued feminist and other critiques relevant to the gendered aspects of modernism, and yet these rich themes continue to be marginalized in many broader syntheses about modernism. This book questions the viability of such a canon without a serious engagement with the gendered aspects—be they limitations or opportunities for a deeper understanding—of the cultural vision and political ethos of modernism. I also posit that one reason for such reluctance is that it is simply much easier to celebrate and especially sell modernist creativity without the critical nuances and the fundamental questioning of the modernist spirit that my approach implies. For, in effect, this study questions the extent to which we can accept the claims made by some of most celebrated modernists that their aesthetic, intellectual, or political vision departed radically from the conditions in which these cultural producers lived.

The uncomfortable reality I wish to make relevant for our understanding of modernism is that many artists who claimed to be part of a radically new avant-garde were in fact, much like the political avant-garde of that period (from Mussolini to Lenin), traditional in their understanding, representation, and performance of gender norms. Questioning established gender roles, even as they explored dreams, alternate realities, eroticism, urbanism, or technology, was not on the agenda for most of the men (and some of the women) active in the modernist movement. That much public discourse on modernism has not yet incorporated gender analyses as a basic consideration of modernist ideas and artifacts only reinforces the need to push against this blind spot and to ask: Who "owns" modernism and for whom?

Modernism is big business in Europe today. It has become a centerpiece of museum displays and many glossy coffee table books, and tours are organized to introduce visitors from other countries and as far away as China to the core achievements of whatever European cultural capital they are visiting. This is nowhere truer than in Brussels, which used to be a rather provincial capital of a small country in Western Europe, until it was fortunate enough to be designated the center of most EU institutions. In addition to the beautiful architectural structures from the medieval and early modern periods, Brussels is fortunate to have had more recent remarkable cultural developments, made visible by the beautiful fin-de-siècle buildings sprinkled around town, along with the colorful murals of various famous cartoon characters, most prominently Tintin.

What modernist art and architecture offer the contemporary observer is a bridge between the world of antiquated artifacts and values—religiously, politically, socially—and the living world we inhabit today. The shift in fin-de-siècle architecture from the pompous to the functional, while retaining elements of style and elegance one sees in Gothic cathedrals, makes it easier to view the transformation embodied by such structures as progress, rather than rupture.

The crowded landscape of a city like Brussels allows the tourist to also perceive the jarring differences between a huge mural of Tintin and the medieval cathedral a block away as a playful palimpsest of all things European, conveniently located in close vicinity, available for exploration without any forced discursive cohesion, architecturally or otherwise. Inside museums, the modernist exhibits make this playfulness readable and offer clues to how one might situate oneself in relation to the radically different styles and cultural values represented by such diverse artifacts. The collage quality, the multiplicity of outputs, the obvious wrestling with form, function, and meaning found in modernist artifacts, provide a wide and comforting pallet to the contemporary visitor.

Everyone can find something to like or be enchanted and challenged by, even as parts of the modernist collections remain on the bizarre side of things, at least as made visible by such exhibits. Thus, as we aim to remind ourselves of the revolutionary quality of modernism, we are confronted with a taming of these works, especially in terms of the art world. Commodification through tourism has pushed the radical and the uncomfortable toward the conventional and the familiar.[5]

The trend in taming modernism deserves further examination in many aspects. This book aims to focus primarily on how modernists interrogated existing gender norms and practices, how those practices and norms themselves generated certain directions in the modernist movements (cultural, intellectual, and political), and how in turn the subsequent scholarship on and commodification of modernism have or have not in fact grappled with these issues. To try and speak to the relationship between modernism and gender in a substantial manner seems like an overwhelming task. If one thinks of gender norms and practices as I do, as an element of human interaction and self-understanding that permeates all areas of individual and social life, then gender is both an omnipresent force and difficult to disentangle from other aspects of modernist thinking, action, and production. Yet it is important to do so, for gender norms is where some of the most fundamental tensions between modernist claims and actions become exposed, and where we become most aware of the difficulty to sustain the narrative that modernism was fundamentally revolutionary in its goals, impulses, and achievements. From a feminist perspective, this claim is difficult to sustain without criticism, especially in terms of how those who are celebrated as canonically modernist treated gender norms and relations.

What this book proposes, then, is to revisit some of the assumptions about what and who is central to the modernist canon and to lay bare what implications such assumptions have for our understanding of how modernism has or has not challenged gender norms and values. From a long-term historical perspective, I offer insights into the following question: Why do we begin to speak of substantial successes in the women's liberation movement only starting in the 1960s, when modernist movements were trying to unchain themselves from the tyranny of the bourgeois world starting six decades earlier, and many women wanted to put their imprint on that movement by challenging patriarchy? My answers will point toward a need to reconsider both fundamental elements of modernism, especially the claim to its revolutionary qualities, as well as the modernist canon, which was built upon the same masculinist understanding of what modernist movements created as their most original and challenging outputs.

Introduction: What Sort of Rebellion?

Modernism has become a word used interchangeably with rebelliousness against late nineteenth-century norms and against the established aesthetics and values of Victorian society. Scholars define it as a radical break with the past and the insistent questioning of the human condition through unprecedented vantage points in the realm of creative activity, from art to music.[1] Aligned with this break is the restlessness of participants in these movements, their constant attempt to reinvent themselves and the world around them. Stability and predictability were to be challenged, and assumptions about what is good questioned. New styles, new ways of organizing the relationship between the conscious, subconscious, and creativity, and new roles for art—from decorative to activist—are the hallmarks of modernism, as touted by many self-identified modernists and subsequently by their critics, adulators, and historians.

There are also more specific definitions of modernism focusing on aesthetics, from distortion to abstraction, as key to understanding the originality of those artists. For instance, Eugene Lunn identifies four relevant practices: "(1) aesthetic self-consciousness; (2) simultaneity, juxtaposition, or 'montage'. . .; (3) paradox, ambiguity, and uncertainty; and (4) 'dehumanization' . . . and the demise of the integrated or 'unified subject'."[2] Other scholars add several more attributes, such as "abstraction and highly conscious artifice, taking us behind familiar reality, breaking away from familiar functions of language and conventions of form . . . the shock, the violation of expected continuities, the element of de-creation and crisis."[3] Yet there is no consensus over any specific element or combination thereof to mark an individual work or person as unmistakingly modernist.

By the beginning of the twenty-first century, modernism has become a word that veers on the useless, given its overuse. By the same token, it has also generated a canon that has been at times celebrated, sometimes contested, but overall accepted as representing the core of the spirit of that age.[4] The growing number of museums dedicated to modernist movements (e.g., the Blue Rider in Munich) and artists (e.g., the Magritte Museum in Brussels), and the retrospectives dedicated to modernism in museums and galleries across the world (e.g., the centenary celebration of the Armory Show) attest to the growing commodification of modernism as both avant-garde and safe for consumption as a mass product. The critiques produced as part of these canonizing exhibits are themselves a tool for commodification of this rebellion, and seldom strike at the heart of the difficulty to reconcile deep paradoxes and incongruities of the movement.[5]

In fact, the spirit of that age was complex and deserves more immersive contextualization, one that places artists and activists squarely in their sociohistorical milieu to better address the question of how much these modernists lived in the spirit of the rebellion they advocated. This book tests the limits of novelty in modernist ideas and artifacts by looking specifically at the sorts of gender regimes modernists adhered to, and how they reconciled their ideas about tradition and innovation, individual self-expression and social norms, with their own choices as gendered human beings. My driving questions are twofold. First, I want to focus on whether the ideas and rebellions fomented by self-identified modernists reached or not into the area of gender norms. Since sexuality and gender relations provided frequent topics in literature, theater, the visual arts, and dance, how modernists drove these themes in radically new directions is my first area of inquiry.[6] My analysis here examines critically the modernist canon and suggests revisions. While modernism encompassed activities and artifacts that profoundly challenged existing gender roles, it also included many movements and works that reinforced and even amplified gender polarization and overall a misogynist view of women without questioning contemporary gender norms.

Second, I present an expanded discussion of structural and discursive contexts that helped shape the gender regimes in which modernists and their contemporaries lived. My analysis focuses on several areas of cultural and political activity that helped articulate the specific obstacles and limitations against which artists, writers, and political activists rebelled. From education to publishing, collecting, and scholarly criticism, women faced significantly different strictures and opportunities at the hands of sexist institutions and practices controlled by men.

Finally, I move from analyzing a number of canonical producers of culture to discussing the actions of artists, thinkers, and activists who rejected traditional gender norms, to ask what other types of activities can be considered modernist. This third part is not exhaustive either, but proposes substantial enhancements of what encompasses modernism.

What I want to advance here is rethinking the modernist canon with gender not as a secondary consideration, outside of the primary analytical frame of the objects, texts, or aesthetics considered, but rather as a fully present framework of analysis. This is first because gender regimes helped shape artistic movements of the late nineteenth and early twentieth centuries. It is also because, given the popularity of the language and images developed by modernist artists, the legacies of these gender regimes are felt until today, not only in the scholarship about the modernist canon, but also in the development of art, design, political movements, and social relations in our own time.[7] Our contemporary sense of aesthetics has clearly been shaped in part by the modernist movement, and our representations of gender norms similarly influenced by these experiments. We owe it to ourselves to look both appreciatively and critically at the assumptions about gender roles embedded in the modernist canon. My conclusions point toward questioning some progressive elements of modernism, while offering suggestions for identifying other democratizing ones.

Modernism: A Definition

I cannot start my analysis without a clear definition of what I understand by modernism and how that compares with the definitions employed by other scholars. For a long time, I took Marshall Berman's definition in *All That Is Solid Melts into Air* as an accurate expression of what I considered unique and relevant for this movement:

> To be modern . . . is to experience personal and social life as a maelstrom, to find one's world and oneself in perpetual disintegration and renewal, trouble and anguish, ambiguity and contradiction: to be part of a universe in which all that is solid melts into air. To be a modernist is to make oneself somehow at home in the maelstrom, to make its rhythms one's own, to move within its currents in search of the forms of reality, of beauty, of freedom, of justice, that its fervid and perilous flow allows.[8]

With this definition, Berman suggested evocatively the messiness that modernist artists brought into the art world and intellectual circles in the late nineteenth century. He highlighted the gendered aspects of modernism: the maelstrom he pointed to above was a force that fueled "an amazing variety of visions and ideas that aim[ed] to make men and women the subjects as well as the objects of modernization, to give them the power to change the world that is changing them, to make their way through the maelstrom and make it their own."[9] He also pointed toward the individualist anti-traditionalist sensibilities that tied many of the disparate efforts of modernist producers of culture. Yet scholars like Rita Felski have critiqued Berman's underlying assumptions about the gender of modernity as masculine and of tradition as feminine, exposing his own masculinist epistemological limitations.[10]

With Roger Griffin and others more recently pushing the boundaries of what this "movement" means and especially any assumptions about the democratizing nature of modernism, the landscape of ideas and actions encompassed by modernism has become more varied.[11] Griffin defines modernism as a way of thinking that "encourages the artist/intellectual to collaborate proactively with collective movements for radical change and projects for the transformation of social realities and political systems."[12] This definition opens up the possibility of looking beyond works of art into performative aspects of social and political activism to broaden the spectrum of modernist rebellion against the past. Equally important is Griffin's interest in identifying modernism with "projects for the transformation of social reality," which in essence raises the bar for how we understand the intentions of these activists and artists in relation to their own actions and works.

If the transformation modernists sought was "total," then by all means our analysis of their actions should encompass the totality of their lives, inclusive of their performance and representation of gender norms. If we ignore the historical context in which Pablo Picasso or Virginia Woolf worked to produce modernist artifacts, we would not offer an analysis that reflects the ethos of the movement they are associated with. By the same token, this significantly enlarged definition of modernism suggests that activities many critics leave outside the framework of analysis should be included in our understanding of this movement. For example, the work of Emma Goldman, who is not included in the modernist canon by most scholars, seems a suitable subject in this larger framework, given her radical ideas in the realm of gender roles, as well as her writing, publications, and performances as a public speaker and anarchist activist.

Along the lines of enlarging the framework of what modernist ideas and activities encompass, Marius Turda has identified eugenics as a modernist movement, focusing on the comprehensive attempt to biologize identity in unprecedented ways and the kind of totalizing view of social engineering most eugenicists favored.[13] My book also takes up considerations about the impact of eugenics in reimagining gender norms and identities, both in sociopolitical activism and in the realm of cultural production.[14] In my definition of modernism, it is the reference to modernism as a "collective movement," as well as the comprehensiveness and radicalness of the change advocated by modernists, that intrigues me the most.

It is important to clarify from the start that my analysis does not have an underlying understanding of modernism as implicitly "progressive," and conversely, that antidemocratic or misogynist views of gender norms could not thus be considered as modernist. The definition above suggests that questioning established values and norms on the part of modernists had both progressive and antidemocratic potentialities. In this broader view, I place feminist activists and ardent supporters of eugenics on the same broad spectrum of modernists who challenged established gender roles and wished to revolutionize how states related to citizens and citizens understood themselves as part of political communities through gendered lenses.

The twin questions I propose to answer with this book are: First, to what extent did self-identified modernists extend the radicalness of their ideas and aesthetic expressions to questions of gender norms? Second, what other individuals and movements that advocated radical change in gender norms and identities should be included in the modernist canon? My analysis is not exhaustive, but it aims instead in shifting the framework of our understanding by accounting more thoroughly for this still often-slighted aspect of the artifacts and actions of people in the modernist movement.

Geographically, though important relevant case studies can be found across the globe, I will focus largely on Europe. There are a few important cases I bring in from North America as well, given the lively trans-Atlantic conversations among many modernists and the impact of many prominent figures from the United States in Mexico in critiquing gender roles in Europe and vice versa. My examples will be derived from both well-known personalities in France, Britain, and Germany, as well as from lesser-known movements and figures in Eastern Europe. The east European cases serve as an important addition to our consideration of modernism, because of the substantially different sociopolitical context of those lands in relation to the more familiar ones in France and Germany. An important component of my argument relates to the meaning of "radicalness" in modernism: we always need to define the expanse of a set of ideas that reject traditions and established norms by looking at the specific context in which these ideas develop. An idea might be very radical in London, but not so in Warsaw, depending on the local traditions, or vice versa. The geographically diverse cases I bring in serve to answer this larger question.

A vast spectrum of activities fits under the umbrella of "collective movements for radical change and projects for the transformation of social realities and political systems," and I will be selective in this regard as well. My choice of individuals and activities is driven specifically by their active engagement with gender norms, from general themes in one's art to subjects toward which self-avowed modernists seemed to gravitate. For those individuals and actions not part of the modernist canon but speaking to the same modernist ethos described above, by addressing specifically the radicalness and transformative power of their actions, I will make the argument for their more thorough inclusion in our consideration of modernism. Still, there is no attempt to be comprehensive here, only evocative and provocative. Including certain individuals also means excluding others, and one can ultimately fault any such framing as too subjective. My answer is that every history of modernism I have read makes a similar set of choices driven by the degree to which the works the author has picked are evocative to her or him.

Finally, a word about timeline. The bookends of modernism seem to be shifting constantly, and there is no good reason to pick any specific starting and ending points along this timeline, other than in relation to the focus of this study on gender norms.[15] One might start with the publication of *Madame Bovary* in 1856, which some deem as the beginning of modernism, and which also focuses squarely on gender norms.[16] However, such an early start would make it impossible to encompass the variety of perspectives and changes that took place in modernist movements in relation to gender norms. Thus, while I reference some of these early precursors, the period I focus predominantly on extends from the 1890s to the 1930s. The tail end of the story is the rise of authoritarian regimes in interwar Europe in the mid-1930s, which ushered in a radically different set of political, economic, and cultural challenges, culminating in the Second World War. This half-century provides ample examples for the beginnings, flourishing, and significant challenges faced by modernists in all the areas of activity covered by this book, or early, high, and late modernism, as many scholars refer to the stages of modernism. To ease the reader's ability to move along the narrative with my characters, my approach to analyzing specific examples is to move chronologically through this period, even though some of the ideas and objects created in any particular period of time did not necessarily converse with each other.

Scholarship on Modernism and Gender[17]

The bulk of the scholarship focusing on the gender dimensions of modernism falls in the area of literary and art criticism, with some important additions from intellectual and cultural historiography. Feminist scholars have made the most significant contributions to both critiquing and augmenting the modernist canon from the perspective of gender analysis.

Until the 1970s, the question of how modernists dealt with gender norms and how gender norms and practices shaped modernist ideas and movements was simply of little interest to most scholars and critics interested in modernism. Voices that pressed for greater focus on these aspects of modernism were present in public discourse from the beginnings of modernist stirrings and especially after the First World War. In *A Room of One's Own*, for instance, Virginia Woolf drew attention to the structural (intellectual, political, and social) obstacles against women's ability to be creative, innovative, and thus make important contributions to cultural production during the modernist period.[18] Yet such voices remained marginal or poorly integrated into larger comprehensive scholarly analyses for a long time.

The modernist canon and scholarship that helped fashion it were shaped in the image of those who wrote about the subject, initially art and literary historians like Milton Brown. Brown wrote the most comprehensive analysis of the Armory Show at its fiftieth anniversary and is also the author of an often-cited history of American modernism.[19] Brown's analysis paid scant attention to any questions of gender, even when they were clearly relevant to understanding the impact of this important moment in the history of modernism, from the presence of women artists in the show (Who? Why? With what impact in the art world?) to the impact of women in funding the show. His analysis of women as fundraisers is particularly telling in terms of lack of curiosity regarding women as historical agents: to not ask why so many of them gave money for this avant-garde unprecedented event significantly diminishes Brown's analysis, given the fact that the show could not have taken place without these women's financial efforts. According to Brown, Arthur B. Davies was the main personality responsible for gathering the financial resources, while the women who brought in the majority of funds that enabled the staging of the exhibit are reduced to "a whole circle of devoted women art patrons."[20] His passing explanation is downright condescending, communicating more about Brown's sexist assumptions regarding historical agency, rather than about modernism and gender in North America in 1913. Nonetheless, Brown's work has continued to be cited as an authoritative analysis of the Armory Show until today.[21]

In the 1970s, with the growing prominence of feminist scholarship in all academic disciplines, the historiography and cultural criticism focusing on the modernist movement started to include a more sustained consideration of questions about gender norms and practices. Initially, these critiques focused first and foremost on the invisibility of women from the modernist canon as creators of culture.[22] Much of the work done during this period was to document the presence of women and to bring a lot more nuance to the structural impediments to women's access to the art world and participation in the public sphere more broadly.

By the mid-1980s, with the poststructuralist turn in historical writing, these explorations widened to considerations of political, social, economic, and cultural networks of power anchoring gender roles. Between Michel Foucault's *History of Sexuality* and Joan Scott's "Gender as a Useful Category of Historical Analysis," more gender studies scholars entered the conversation about what characterized modernism; what the politics of various modernists were; and how did identity, gender norms, and forms of intellectual or social action impact each other during this period of cultural experimentation and political radicalism.[23] This is the period when biographies, specialized studies, as well as bold anthologies and syntheses began to situate women more front and center in the scholarship on modernism, and also opened up new areas of inquiry regarding gender norms more broadly.[24]

During the 1990s we also see the beginning of scholarship addressing the relationship between modernism and masculinity.[25] With the question of gender norms opened up to comprehensive criticism, historians and other scholars began to ask how masculinity was shaped by modernism, and how self-understandings of masculinity shaped the critiques and innovations that male modernist artists and activists produced. It is in fact striking to see the extent to which *Modernism/modernity*, a journal that began publication in 1994 and is dedicated to the exploration of modernism, writ large, has focused on questions about masculinity when engaging with "gender" more broadly.[26]

The queering of scholarship on modernism started also during this period, under the influence of Foucault and especially Judith Butler.[27] This field of inquiry developed by initially making visible the heteronormative assumptions of earlier scholarship, and subsequently providing important new nuances for our appreciation of the innovations and limitations of modernist artists, writers, film makers, etc.[28] By focusing on the intersectionality of gender, sexuality, and increasingly race, such works have also fundamentally altered our understanding of canonical movements and artifacts during this period of rebellion.

The proliferation of so many flavors of gender analysis enables us to critique older narratives about modernism as lacking awareness of and interest in interrogating this fundamental aspect of human activity. However, it is also clear that some recent syntheses of modernism have continued to find it unimportant to thoroughly integrate gender analysis in their revisiting of modernism over a century after the movement started. The centenary of the Armory Show provides a useful example in this regard. The large and beautiful volume brought out by the New York Historical Society for the retrospective exhibit held in 2013 features one article on feminism at the Armory Show. Charles Musser's chapter provides extremely useful information about the women participants in the show, their connections with the men exhibiting and the organizers, as well as women's access to the established and newer art associations at that time.[29] It is somewhat of a corrective to Brown's silence. However, the issues the article engages with have bearing on other topics in the volume, and there is no effort on the part of the editors or other authors to engage with these questions. In short, gender analysis is reduced to a brief exploration of feminism and to mentioning in passing the feminist allegiances of a few of the people involved in the show. By contrast, a more recent study focusing squarely on the women involved in every aspect of the Armory Show, from exhibiting to fundraising and collecting, provides an excellent example of the important insights we can gain into understanding the meaning of modernism and its long-term impact through a thorough gender analysis of the subject.[30]

At the same time, there are clear signs that greater interest in gender analysis is taking hold of scholarship on modernism. One revealing relatively new publication is the journal *Modernist Cultures*, which was started in Edinburgh in 2005.[31] In its first decade, or nineteen issues that appeared before August 2015, the journal included thirty-six research articles with discussions of gender, of which twenty-four referred to masculinity as well. Discussion of women's issues has been more frequent, however, with sixty-six such articles.[32] Though this may seem like a crass quantitative analysis, the frequency with which questions about gender, women, or masculinity appear in this journal suggests that the editors of this journal have an abiding interest in gendering modernism.

Organization of the Book

My exploration of modernism and gender is divided into three parts. In the first two chapters I offer a gender analysis of important examples from the modernist canon, with an eye to enhancing our appreciation for these works and individuals in terms of the degree of innovation they articulated in the area of reflecting on gender roles. My goal is two-pronged: to begin with, I offer a feminist critique of the gendered limitations present in some of the iconic figures of modernism, such as Pablo Picasso or André Breton. At the same time, I provide an appreciative discussion of works in the modernist canon that have not been the focus of much gender analysis, even though they challenged the established gender roles of the day. Charlie Chaplin's films are a particularly significant case study.

Next I explore how the modernist canon was shaped, focusing on three areas of inquiry: (1) access or the gendered institutional limitations to participating in public activism, art education, and publication during the half-century encompassed in this book; (2) visibility, or who collected and thus rendered valuable specific modernist works, and whose works sold well and became financially valuable; and (3) scholarship, or how did the canon come into being and change over time. This chapter connects the process by which we have come to signify modernism to these three sets of contexts that I consider essential for fully appreciating why gender analysis is still not fully integrated in many histories of modernism.

Finally, I turn my attention to movements and works that are unevenly identified as modernist, to suggest why and how we need to think of them as significant in terms of questioning and making an effort to upend gender norms.

I focus first on psychology, sexology, eugenics, and nudism as disciplines and movements, respectively, that aimed to fundamentally rearticulate gender identity and norms, and highlight the work of several important cases and some lesser-known examples. In the second part of this chapter I focus on anarchism, communism, and fascism as modernist movements that do not focus primarily on questioning gender roles, but whose contributions to reframing gender norms and expectations are very significant and need to be more fully integrated in the scholarship on modernism. This organizational structure is two pronged: it aims to critique assumptions about and analyses of modernism that do not pay attention to gender; it also enhances our understanding of what modernism was (or failed to become), if gender is to be an essential element of scholarly analysis of the movement. I hope to show that much is to be gained in nuance, connections between artists and activists, the array of creative innovative expressions associated with modernism, as well as the links between the works and actions of these remarkable men and women and our own gender sensibilities today.

1

Modernism before the Great War

In the late nineteenth century, as European empires and the United States were celebrating their great expansion overseas and advances in civilization and technology, not to mention the growth of capitalist economy, a number of social movements and artistic groupings signaled dissatisfaction with these successes and demanded in no uncertain terms the upending of the current world order. Some of the discontented voices belonged to those who wanted to have a seat at the table of plenty, such as the nationalist movements in the Habsburg or Ottoman Empires. Others focused on deeper problems of racism, sexism, and economic inequality, and wished to see them acknowledged and eliminated. For these critics, the seats and the table were to be refashioned. Others, more radically, wished to eliminate deeper traditions, from organized religion to well-established social institutions, such as the family and marriage. What shape and relationships would emerge after tearing down the current edifices was not a concern among some of these radical thinkers and activists; they simply viewed a rotten mess of structures that needed to be eradicated; and other radical critics envisioned a new world order. Modernism emerged out of these various voices and over time developed its own ideological and aesthetic vocabularies. In turn, these new forms of self-expression impacted the direction and goals of the social and political movements in which modernist thinkers and artists participated.

It was during this period that challenges to gender norms began to gain prominence in public discourse, in everything from politics to culture. Supporters of women's rights began to organize internationally and develop activist networks.[1] Advocates for women's education were seeing signs of encouragement on the part of the emerging Parliamentary regimes throughout Europe, at least at the precollegiate level. In industrialized economies women were starting to have a significant presence on the factory floor. And though abuses continued, women did benefit from some activism on behalf of restricting the workday for women and children. Migration to the growing metropolitan centers in Europe and North America also altered the landscape of the city, especially as transportation eased access to long distances.[2] More young women than ever before hopped on trains from their small towns and villages and made their way to the alluring bright lights and opportunities on offer in big cities. These dynamic processes led to greater expectations and frustrations and eventually laid the groundwork for questioning the established political and social order, as well as the values and culture undergirding them, inclusive of gender roles.

Awakenings: Early Modernist Experiments

One of the earliest rebellions took place among writers against the literary bourgeois canon and its celebration of linear progress and family values. Novelists played a crucial role here, as the novel had become a widespread form of reading, popularized even further by the development of serial publications in inexpensive newspapers read by people across the socioeconomic spectrum.[3] From Gustave Flaubert to Kate Chopin, a number of prominent novelists used this beloved form to introduce unorthodox takes on themes of broad sociocultural relevance. Playwrights such as Henrik Ibsen were equally important for translating these critiques into a visual aesthetic that was performative and deeply disquieting to the audiences who expected to be entertained rather than challenged when they dressed up for a night on the town. These authors' understanding of the existing gender regimes and their challenges of these norms formed an important component of the thematic spectrum of this wave of literary discontent.

The publication of Flaubert's *Madame Bovary* (1856) and Chopin's *The Awakening* (1899), as well as the premiere of Ibsen's *A Doll's House* (1879), provoked immediate uproar.[4] The vitriolic reactions in the press demonstrate the discomfort these works caused for the reading public and literary critics, for whom it was precisely the subject of independent female sexuality and social agency, as well as the specific features of the female characters, taking on roles that moved them outside of the prescription of Victorian gender norms, that troubled the sensibilities of their contemporaries. Some actresses refused to play Nora in the staging of *A Doll's House*, citing their discomfort with impersonating a woman who would leave her husband and children.[5] Even though the role was rich and provided an avenue for great acting, somehow it was unacceptable even for artists whose craft was tied to pretending. At the early showings of the play in Denmark, Britain, France, and the United States, the public also reacted with various degrees of shock and displeasure, sometimes walking out in the middle of a scene. The work of Ibsen and Flaubert quickly became known in the rest of Europe. *A Doll's House* premiered in Warsaw in 1882 and played there to full houses before the North American and British public were ready to take in the play as it had been written.[6] Today, we look at literature or films with a heroine who does not wish to marry, gets divorced, or refuses to assume the role of mother in a marriage, as commonplace. A hundred and twenty-five years ago, such portraits were beyond the pale of social respectability.

These literary works, and others like them, provoked discomfort also because of the settings in which women's actions were placed. Everything in the setting was recognizable to the reader: the traditions, the language, and the structures that regulated their own lives. And yet, the reactions of the main female characters fell out of that familiar universe, and the reader was asked to understand those unfamiliar reactions and in some instances to empathize with characters displaying this unfamiliar behavior. Instead of literary pleasure, one experienced disorientation or aggravation, unless one happened to be predisposed already toward empathizing with an emancipated female character. The tragic turn in these works came not from the failure of the female characters to observe the social mores of the day at the expense of their own social standing. It came from the impossibility of reconciling the existing mores with the desires of that character, which were not rendered moral or amoral by the author in accordance with existing gender norms.

These portraits of rational, fully empowered women who found themselves frustrated or simply silenced by the society in which they lived, challenged important orthodoxies of the day, which we need to remember in order to fully appreciate the challenge this literature posed to the existing gender norms. Most European civil codes of the day took marriage to be a fundamental norm and placed married women in a position of economic and legal dependency.[7] Women could gain full legal autonomy and economic power only as widows, or if they chose not to marry, which placed them in a socially marginal position. In some parts of Europe, the Napoleonic Code adopted in the course of the nineteenth century included interdictions against women signing any contracts on their own and women concluding contracts with men, and against married women's freedom to live in a location of their choice or to travel to and stay overnight in places their husbands had not given them permission to go.[8]

Thus, when, toward the end of *A Doll's House*, Nora states that "I was simply transferred from papa's hands into yours [her husband's]," she is just voicing a legal fact, the dirty open secret about women's legal subjection to men that struck at the core of gender norms in Victorian Europe. She continues more pointedly:

> You arranged everything according to your own taste, and so I got the same tastes as you—or else I pretended to, I am really not quite sure which—I think sometimes the one and sometimes the other. When I look back on it, it seems to me as if I had been living here like a poor woman—just from hand to mouth. I have existed merely to perform tricks for you, Torvald. But you would have it so. You and papa have committed a great sin against me. It is your fault that I have made nothing of my life.[9]

This climactic scene, for which many audiences were unprepared in 1879, gets to the bottom of what bourgeois society was based on—the two-tier gender regimes of the day, which subjected women to profound forms of injustice.

Uttering these facts exposed sexism for what it was and suggested unambiguously the need to end these restrictions, or women would simply walk out of this contract. One cannot overstate the impact of Ibsen's work in opening up new intellectual debates regarding women's position in society, as well as a host of new possibilities for articulating women's voices on stage. A decade after the premiere, Emma Goldman pointed toward Ibsen and Nora in particular as the iconic voice of the Victorian "doll" and a powerful argument on the side of rejecting marriage as a form of oppression of all women by all men.[10]

Nora's words also strike at the heart of the aesthetics of late nineteenth-century Europe. When she says "you arranged everything according to your taste," the audience could easily look around and see, beyond the edifice of women's ornate fashions and the well-appointed bourgeois homes, a set of norms and aesthetic options that were constructed by men for men, with women as their dolls rather than partners in building a society and lives together. Ibsen's critique advocated for moving in the direction of emancipated partnership, though few were willing to follow at that time. But his critique initiated a cry to mobilize the public toward both eradicating existing values and aesthetic forms and constructing different gender norms that would inform what beauty and harmony would mean, based on mutual pleasure and active participation by both partners in a marriage. In this future world, women would gain full autonomy as subjects and historical agents, shaping their surroundings according to their own sensibilities, rather than men's. One can go so far as to say that Ibsen called for an emboldening of female subjectivity and autonomy as necessary conditions for the flourishing of modernity.

In Great Britain, important challenges to women's second-class-citizen status were afoot, and they provided important counterexamples elsewhere in Europe to the Napoleonic Code's limitations of married women's legal status. Between 1870 and 1880, the British Parliament passed two important laws that eliminated married women's coverture and established them as sole legal entities, able to control their property and enter or exit contracts without their husband's permission.[11] Yet it took many more years of activism and a world war for other states in Europe to catch up to these changes in Britain. In France, for instance, women gained full legal and political rights only after the Second World War.

Around the same time as these changes were taking place in Victorian England, Oscar Wilde published *The Portrait of Dorian Gray* (1890), which scandalized the readership so much, that the author felt compelled to revise the novel and provide an explanatory introduction to it the following year.[12] Wilde's work reflected critically and unapologetically on contemporary gender norms, as well as on the view of art in Britain as having to serve a social purpose or be morally inspiring in order to have value. Wilde's homoeroticism, both in the novel and in real life, offended the notions of masculinity and propriety accepted in Victorian society. For not only were women to be married and supportive of their husbands, but men were to be married and protect their wives, for the benefit of society at large. Wilde's refusal to play by these rules and instead follow his desires was too much for the respectable society to bear, especially given his public prominence and close relations with some among the English aristocracy; he paid for his choices with imprisonment and dire poverty. If he became a pariah in the aristocratic and bourgeois circles in London, his trial and imprisonment turned Wilde into a cause celèbre for the gay movement, and influenced bohemian modernists on both sides of the Atlantic.[13]

The most important challenge in Wilde's work, however, was not the expression of his homosexual preferences, but rather the unabashed aestheticism at the core of *Dorian Gray*:

> One's own life—that is the important thing. As for the lives of one's neighbors, if one wishes to be a prig or a Puritan, one can flaunt one's moral views about them, but they are not one's concern. Besides, Individualism has really the higher aim. Modern morality consists in accepting the standard of one's age. I consider that for any man of culture to accept the standard of his age is a form of the grossest immorality. . . . As for being poisoned by a book, there is no such thing as that. Art has no influence upon action. It annihilates the desire to act. It is superbly sterile. The books that the world calls immoral are books that show the world its own shame.[14]

Wilde acclaims individualism and aestheticism above concerns with morality (and implicitly gender norms) as framed by his contemporaries. He wants to establish art as a space for celebrating pleasure and the freedom to flaunt moral codes, completely divorced from social responsibility. And he chooses to express his aestheticism through both writing and personal sexual preferences.

Wilde's homosexuality thus became a means for acting according to pleasure and aesthetics above social norms, because "to accept the standard of [one's] age is a form of grossest immorality." For Wilde, authenticity and beauty were connected to one's individual sexual desires and not the prescriptions of one's contemporaries; embracing those desires and expressing one's joy and sorrows in relation to them was the only position an authentic artist could take.

The aestheticist positioning exemplified by Wilde was an important early strand of modernist thinking and art. When he expressed his desire to divorce art from any social purpose, Wilde's perspective connected closely with that of the pre-Raphaelites, especially the ideas of John Ruskin.[15] Of course, the very statement that "art has no influence upon action. It annihilates the desire to act," actually had enormous sway over other artists of his generation and into the future; it generated new avenues for self-expression and for imagining gender roles that fell outside accepted norms. This elitist antipolitical version of rebelling against Victorian social norms became a second important stream of art and action in the modernist movement at the turn of the century, antithetical to the call for action and overt social critiques espoused by other modernists, such as Ibsen.

To fully appreciate the range of perspectives aestheticists developed regarding gender roles, I turn my gaze toward *Salomé*, both the Wilde play and the theme of Salomé among the modernist poets, composers, and artists of the last years of the nineteenth century.[16] Building on the work of others, such as Flaubert, Wilde rendered the character of Salomé a powerful iconic figure that reverberates until today in art, music, theater, dance, and poetry. Wilde's play brought Salomé herself at the center of the story and turned her into a symbol of female sexuality and iconic object of masculine anxieties. Many aspects of this character signal a rejection of certain gender norms, most prominently Salomé's own voice and self-assuredness as a sexual being, which violated respectable norms for women at that time. Her desires were represented unabashedly as a force to be reckoned with; she was the mistress of her own body and wielded it as a powerful weapon. Her actions were not subservient to those of her mother, but rather guided by her own will, and aligned with Wilde's own view of beauty—devoid of any considerations of morality.

If in *Dorian Gray* Wilde provided an empathetic description of male homoerotic desires, his portrait of Salomé depicted female sexuality as threatening to men and ultimately deadly. The commentary provided by *Salomé* on gender norms was rather unrebellious, when it came to Wilde's view of women's sexuality and historical agency: their embrace was emasculating and potentially deadly, and to gaze upon them was to commit suicide. His view of women's roles in relation to men was diametrically opposed to the portrait provided by Ibsen, who called into question the power relations between men and women as enshrined by society and the legal constrictions of the nineteenth century. As an aestheticist, Wilde was uninterested in such contexts; by taking a biblical story and turning it into a play that combined contemporary artistic themes with his own preoccupation with desire, power, and beauty, he chose to essentialize this polarized dynamic of gender relations, and to render the masculine anxieties of his contemporaries into a universalizing trope about women's threatening sexual agency.

An important additional element of this play in articulating new representations of gender roles is the Orientalizing of racialized features of the story and of Salomé herself. The setting, costumes, and famous dance of the seven veils all evoked images of a lascivious Orient, of a sexuality that was both exotic and threatening. A West European viewer might take some solace in watching the play because the discomfort presented by *Salomé* came in the form of a woman dressed in shalvari, who belonged to a place and culture far removed from Western Europe at the turn of the century.

For others, this Orientalist trope may have presented the most alluring element of the story. Fascination with the exotic "other" had grown during Europe's colonial expansion ever since the early modern period and especially over the nineteenth century, when the consumption of luxury items, from silk to opium and pornographic art, was spreading from the elites to the middle classes.[17] By the 1890s, artistic themes that entwined eroticism with "the Orient" were common, but it was the centrality of the Salomé character, and especially her unabashed sexualized persona that rendered her a new iconic representation of "the Oriental."

Salomé became an obsessive theme for many artists and writers at the turn of the century. One scholar puts the number of poetic works from this period dedicated to Salomé at over 2,800, and identifies the source of inspiration for many of them in Wilde's play.[18] Clearly, Wilde hit a nerve with his contemporaries in the artistic world in a way that Ibsen did not. Why? Part of the answer may lie with the ambivalence present in the text of *Salomé* and then exploited more fully by others, such as the artist and Wilde's friend Aubrey Beardsley, in his illustrations included with the 1907 edition of the play.[19] The dialogue in the play builds a series of possible further interpretations of Salomé's symbolism, from an identification with the artist, a sort of alter ego for Wilde himself, to her identification with John the Baptist, represented most strikingly in one of Beardsley's illustrations, in which Salomé's face looks like her victim's, once she has his lifeless head on a platter (Figure 1).

Critics have suggested that this ambivalence about Salomé's symbolism encouraged playfulness and appropriation, as well as a certain adoption of her character by the symbolists.[20] That playfulness can be seen in the stagings of

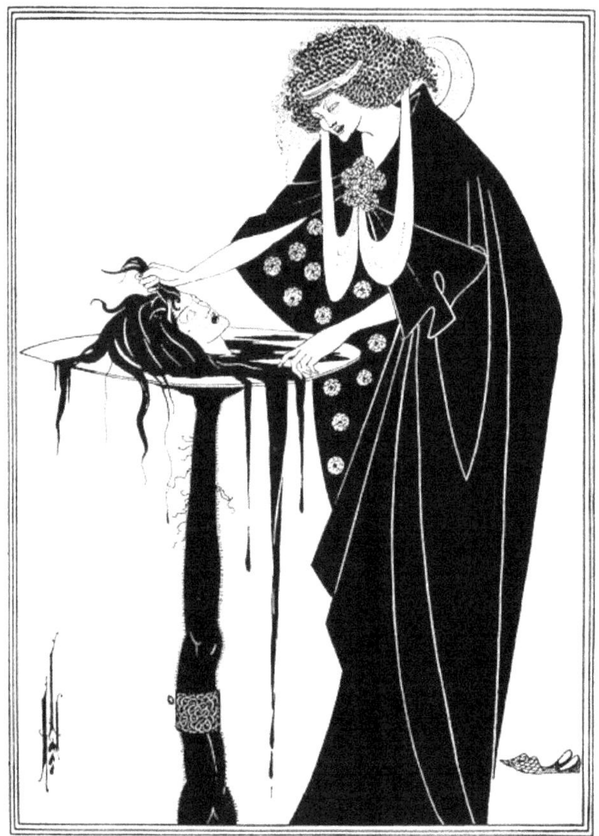

FIGURE 1 *Aubrey Beardsley, "The Dancer's Reward," in Oscar Wilde,* Salomé. A Tragedy in One Act. *London: John Lane, 1893, opposite p. 56.*

Salomé a decade later, when male performers sometimes played the role of the dancer.[21] However, the ending of the play, and Wilde's own words, "Kill that woman!" leave little room for ignoring the undercurrent of misogyny in the play. Salomé was not represented as a victim, but rather as a creative and destructive spirit, whose force rested in elements of femininity commonly associated with danger at that time. Ultimately, those clichés are not turned on their head; instead, they remained the currency in which Wilde still traded as he developed Salomé's character:

> Her "subjectivity" is in fact an expanded projection of the male gaze disguised as the moon-like virgin. As the aesthete with the active eye, she has fulfilled her moon-like ability to transform shapes. But as the woman "looking for dead things," she also holds the shape . . . of an indifferent, dangerous, feminine "nature."[22]

If *Salomé* provided an important resource for reinventing misogyny in a new aesthetic key, Wilde's performance of homosexuality did introduce a radical challenge against Victorian gender norms. Without setting out to become a political activist, he stood up to the heterosexism of his contemporaries and paid dearly for it. His trial and prison sentence turned Wilde into a cause celèbre in the emerging gay movement. He singlehandedly brought into circulation a new aesthetic that was political despite his claims to the contrary. Wilde articulated a vocabulary and aesthetic that helped bring into being performative sexual-identity politics. His impact on the emerging gay culture was almost instantaneous and far-reaching. During the First World War, Habsburg prisoners of war, kept in captivity in Siberia by the Russian imperial forces, staged male-only performances of *Salomé*, using Wilde's text as a means of expressing their sexual frustrations and fantasies both on and off stage.[23]

Fin-de-Siècle: Ends and Beginnings

During the last years of the nineteenth century and in the decade after 1900, the visual arts saw an explosion of creativity and new styles pushing the boundaries of representation and the aesthetic toward more radical changes. The styles that developed during this period were influenced by important changes taking place in the world of science. From the 1870s and until the beginning of the First World War, the Darwinian turn in biology gave rise to eugenics, psychology, and sexology, as branches of scientific inquiry.

The rise of psychology as a new science inspired new ways of experimenting with fiction writing in the 1880s. Henry James and Kate Chopin herself, in the *Awakening*, had started to develop new narrative forms that focused on interior dialogue and the tension between perception and fact as a central element of exploring humanity, inclusive of gender roles. Friedrich Nietzsche had already penned a provocative theory about the irrational in human development.[24] But it was the generation of doctors with deep interest in understating dreams, irrational fears, and the subconscious, who opened up entirely new paths for understanding the relationship between physiological phenomena and irrational impulses, for redrawing the relationship between reason and emotion.

Though initially read by few outside his immediate scientific and personal circles, Sigmund Freud's *Interpretation of Dreams* (1900) became one of the influential texts in defining Freud's understanding of gender differences in the realm of both the subconscious and specifically sexuality.[25] Among other relevant topics, in this book Freud developed the concept of the

"Oedipal complex." Freud's ideas became more broadly known to the non-German speaking world after he was invited to the United States in 1909 to receive an honorary degree, and as his work was being translated into English or used by his disciples in England and over the Atlantic.[26]

Freud's understanding of female sexuality greatly influenced how subsequent generations of modernists engaged with gender norms and identity. His ideas about gender identity and sexuality were rooted in the belief that the male psyche and physiology were the "norm" or normal, while the female body and psyche represented a version of the male, or a derivation, to be more precise. Thus, even as Freud formulated novel theories about how individuals came to act as adults on the basis of psychological and sexual predispositions related to gender, his ideas were founded on traditional masculinist assumptions about gender identity.[27]

Freud's ideas on sexuality received serious criticism from the moment they were published. Phallocentrism, a term coined by Ernest Jones during the same period, offered a fundamental critique of Freud's assumptions about male and female sexuality, with one being the norm (male) and the other derivative (the female).[28] Jones and others, among them Karen Horney, argued that female sexuality and psychology should be understood as rooted in women's unique specificities, not only in relation to men's physiology and women's relation with men. For all his pioneering significance in framing psychoanalytical discourse, Freud espoused assumptions about women's identities that seemed rooted more in biblical text and Victorian notions of female gender roles, rather than in the modernist spirit of rejecting those values and on behalf of an individualist understanding of the self. Freud's ideas about gender, sexuality, and the psyche are probably one of the most long-lasting and impactful legacies of this modernist canonical figure. His writing played a prominent role in how subsequent generations of other modernist thinkers, writers, artists, and activists represented gender relations, most prominently the surrealists starting in the 1920s.

Around the same period, out of networks that intersected with Freud's, came the discipline of sexology, whose pioneering days were also in Austria-Hungary. Starting in the 1870s, in parallel with the biomedical work being done by the followers of Francis Galton in the budding discipline of eugenics, Richard von Krafft-Ebing published work that sought to catalogue sexual behavior according to a number of bio-psychological characteristics and to integrate the understanding of sexual behavior as a core component of medicine.[29] His theories identified both what sexual "normal" behavior was and what types of behavior fell outside that norm. He sought to explain the causes of such behavior by focusing both on physical features and on psychological aspects, and placed these elements in a larger eugenicist framework that included clear binary definitions of gender roles. Sexual and gender norms were the result of an evolutionary process that needed to be tended to through education and also criminalization of the deviant, for abnormal behavior was considered to be a threat both to oneself and to the present and future of the community in which one lived.

With sexology, Krafft-Ebing created both a brand new area of science research and a new basis for reinforcing the Victorian restrictive views on sexuality dominant at that time. His ideas rejected individual freedom as a basis for acting and relating to others, and instead reinforced the notion that individual behavior needed to be weighed against what he and other eugenicists understood as the "common good," a sort of intergenerational hereditary responsibility toward the future rather than just the past and present. This eugenicist mobilization on behalf of ideas about health and the well-being of society is what Turda identifies as an important modernist aspect of eugenics.[30]

The contribution of sexology to modernism is manifold, and I will have more to say about it in Chapter 4. The medicalization of sexual behavior and the development of the concept of sexual identity led to new frameworks for imagining the self and expressing individual desires and anxieties. The topic of sexual behavior itself gained respectability, moving from the realm of prurience and pornography to the pages of medical journals and, before long, sex advice columns. Women, in particular, were interested in reading about their own sexuality as something natural and beautiful, rather than the marital obligation one never spoke of in polite company. Sex advice books made their appearance and greatly changed the norms of decency when it came to written expression about women's sexuality. Over the next decade, books that featured heroines with a well-articulated sex life became mainstream reading material.

Still, even though important barriers in terms of women's sexuality were broken at that time, many sexologists, Kraft-Ebing among them, wished to reinforce the heterosexual norms of the day and provided new arguments for the criminalization of homosexuality.[31] Overall, eugenicists expressed interest in the reproduction of "healthy" populations above all other criteria for valuing sexual behavior. If sex was primarily about reproduction and only secondarily about pleasure, all nonreproductive type of sexual behavior could be valuable only if it led to reproduction. Whatever sex act did not lead to the reproduction of "genetically healthy" populations was deemed by definition abnormal and anti-eugenic. In short, eugenicists viewed all sex that was not copulation between a man and a woman with the male ejaculating inside the woman as biopolitically irresponsible.[32]

The polarized view of sexual behavior that corresponded to eugenicist notions of proper femininity and masculinity aligned a great deal with the Victorian morals of the day, though it also introduced important changes.

While sexologists of this school defined a "normal" woman as having soft curvy shapes, a nonaggressive demeanor, and displaying no facial or arm hair, they also approved of women having a sexual drive that encouraged reproduction. By the same token, these sexologists defined female sexual aggression (for instance, the provocative dress and behavior of sex workers), as well as sexual homoerotic appearance and behavior as "inversions," dangerous to women's own reproductive system as well as a threat to the future of humanity. A similar unforgiving contrast between proper masculine behavior—aggressive and heterosexual versus effeminate and homosexual—defined men's "normal" sexuality. For both men and women, any deviation from normative heterosexuality was also connected to mental or psychological deficiencies, some of which sexologists believed could be corrected, while others were deemed hereditarily dangerous. Reproduction, and by extension fully sanctioned sexual activity, were to be reserved to those who did not present a hereditary danger.

The sexualization of public discourses about morality and the common good around the turn of the century was facilitated both by new science theories and research and by the works of art and literature that showed a preoccupation with these notions of pleasure, common good, and rejection of established gender norms. Alongside Freud, Gustav Klimt and the Secession group he helped found in Vienna in 1897 created a new visual vocabulary for depicting sexual intimacy, entwining nature and the social, and revisiting romantic sensibilities from an ironic perspective. Many of the turn-of-the-century art movements in Europe showed a distinct interest in nature, in decorative organic aesthetics that integrated the work of art into the larger environment, and in blending a variety of traditions of both high and folk art into the visual language of the movement. The Secession group, for instance, used many Japanese traditional techniques in dyeing, printing, and overall composition of the art object, introducing the blank space and the yin-yang balance of Japanese art into their own style.[33] In Cracow, Polish painters used themes from Polish folklore to depict allegorical scenes in large-scale public art projects.[34]

The human body, as a force of nature and symbol of strength and beauty, was a common feature of this artwork. Among the many versions of the turn-of-the-century depictions of human sexuality, none is as famous as Klimt's *Kiss*, whose status has shifted in the past two decades from iconic art object to omnipresent tchotchke. A lesser-known, but equally important, work on this theme was *Jurisprudence*, a massive painting commissioned for the ceiling of the Faculty of Law at the University of Vienna. Comparing the two allows us to see the sort of playfulness that became characteristic of the artists of this time. *Jurisprudence* was executed between 1899 and 1907 as part of a triptych that included *Medicine* and *Philosophy*, and was met with vocal

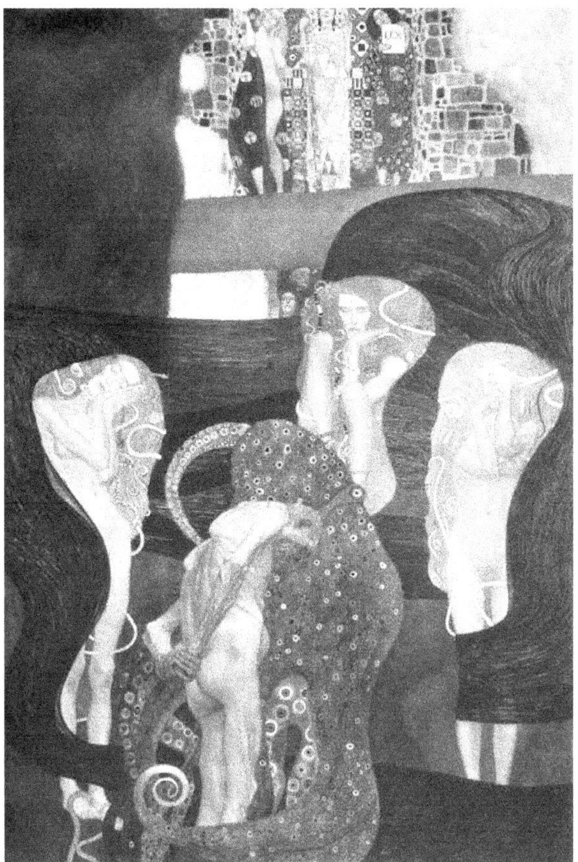

FIGURE 2 *Gustav Klimt,* Jurisprudence. *1907.*

criticism by the conservative voices at the university, who considered Klimt's depictions as cruel and pornographic.[35]

For his depiction of humanity in relation to law, medicine, and philosophy, Klimt opted for nude bodies as conveyors of both truth and beauty above any social convention, a philosophical perspective he adopted from Nietzsche.[36] The male bodies in these paintings have none of the power, the glory, or the beauty that female bodies display. They seem weighed down by the symbolic figures who stand above them—law, life, wisdom—all depicted as women with a penetrating and arresting presence. *Jurisprudence* is a collection of furies, whose foreboding and detached gaze dominate the male figure below. Their hair entwined with snakes reminds one of the terrifying Medusa more than the wise Athena. Standing above in the distance are another three clothed female figures, whose distance and erect posture further clarify the gendered power relations between the naked male figure at the center bottom and the world in which he functions. *Medicine* and *Philosophy* featured similar depictions of humanity as powerless at the feet of these greater forces, rather than conquering them, with the symbolic powerful figures always represented as female, both beautiful and threatening.

Klimt's representation of these disciplines illustrates his modernist interpretation of Nietzschean critiques against religion and Klimt's own skepticism of humanity's triumph over nature. In Klimt's depiction, the sciences are as frail as humanity itself, and as much subject to doubt and failure as the naked man standing at the bottom of *Jurisprudence*. It was this gendered image of frailty and failure that upset the academic establishment more than anything else, as Klimt's vision challenged directly and very visibly the stability of the intellectual discourses of the day and suggested that crisis and failure better characterized European society in 1900 than the solid academic edifices in which knowledge was being taught.[37]

As for the specific gender aspects of how Klimt chose to depict power relations—with the realm of the symbolic and ideas through female bodies, and the realm of humanity through a mix of masculine and feminine figures—one needs to look for interpretive clues at Klimt's visual vocabulary more broadly. Whether nude or clothed, symbolic or human, the female subjects in Klimt's work are constantly a celebration of the female form as beautiful and almost magical. *The Kiss*, his best-known painting, represents love as a glorious heterosexual union of man and woman, the two entangled as one through a golden mélange of flowers, vines, circles, and squares. The phallic form of this tower of love and the man's protecting embrace make it clear that, while complementary, the union of the two is not an equal partnership, but rather a conquest and victory of masculine prowess.[38] Thus, Klimt allows himself to be somewhat traditional in his celebration of love, while also providing powerful and foreboding portraits of female figures. The anxieties and sense of masculinity in crisis that pervades Wilde's representation of gender roles is not as unambiguously present in Klimt. His depiction of women does not communicate the same unavoidable sense of female sexuality and agency as a deadly threat to men's gender roles and desires.

The move after 1900 toward a more complex visual vocabulary in the realm of gender roles is best represented by the work of Pablo Picasso, whose beginnings were contemporary to Klimt's period of controversy and glory. Picasso's *Les Demoiselles d'Avignon* (1907), which has elicited as much fascination as Klimt's *Kiss*, is considered by many art historians as the birth of cubist art. The painting is also a provocative and multifaceted representation of female sexuality and of Picasso's own anxieties about women. The origins and meaning of the painting have been subject to intense debate since its first public viewing in 1916, and some critics assign it far more specific personal meaning (e.g., the link between Picasso contracting syphilis around that time and the menacing and empty look of two of the faces on the right side of the painting) than can be demonstrated without any doubt.[39]

Les Demoiselles depicts a group of five sex workers from a brothel Picasso used to frequent in Barcelona. The name was changed at the time of the painting's first showing to prevent a scandalized reception. Picasso made different choices and offered various degrees of abstractness in representing the five female figures, one of the reasons the painting elicited so much interest from the start. The faces of the three women on the left are closer to a recognizable physiognomy, though their eyes are vacant. The two figures on the right are more mask-like and were inspired by Picasso's interest in African art and primitivism, which was a growing current in modernist art in Paris at that time.[40] Harmony and any conventional depiction of female sexuality as beautiful are absent from this painting. The vacant eyes of the women on the left seem both sad and foreboding, and the mask-like faces on the right move even further toward provoking puzzlement and discomfort. Sex is denuded from a link to temptation, pleasure, or satisfaction. The cubist forms adopted by Picasso break down any such correlation and instead force the viewer to figuratively step back and react to the painting both in a more intellectual vein and also more emotionally, though outside the realm of voyeuristic gazing. Color and line provide a new abstract vocabulary for conveying Picasso's own anxieties, turning on their head traditional assumptions about and tropes regarding perspective, color, light, shading, or the human body itself.

Some critics have concluded that *Les Demoiselles* shows Picasso's "deep-seated fear and loathing of the female body, which existed side by side with his craving for and ecstatic idealization of it."[41] Whether the painting provoked a similar response from viewers or elicited other interpretations, this statement illustrates important elements of the modernist approaches to gender roles at the turn of the century: contradictory views coexisted in the same frame, eschewing unitary meaning; the potency of sexuality as a subject in art grew with the rejection of the moral codes and masks of restrained harmony of the late nineteenth century; and images of the female body became a vehicle for communicating a multiplicity of emotions, rather than necessarily the representation of female subjectivity itself.

Picasso's influence on some contemporaries was remarkable and his own body of work produced a myriad of other paintings, drawings, and sculptures with some of the same themes and approach to women's bodies and gender relations. Yet other artists from the same Parisian circles approached the subject from very different vantage points and used different stylistic tools. The Romanian-born Constantin Brâncuşi used simplicity in abstraction and primitivism to celebrate sexuality and beauty in both a poetic and playfully ironic way, sometimes in the same piece. His style has been defined by some as Platonic (for instance, his series of sculptures for the blind, meant to be experienced through touch rather than seeing), yet it also focused on earthy subjects throughout his entire artistic life, from the male and female body to sexuality and pleasure.[42]

The work of Brâncuși represents an important milestone in the development of a new visual vocabulary for signifying gender roles precisely because of the level of abstraction and simplicity he reached in depicting gendered themes.[43] This simplicity became a door toward multiple and sometimes contradictory readings of Brâncuși's vision about gender roles and especially sexuality. By freeing the public from identifying femininity and masculinity along any unambiguous power relations, he offered a new set of tools to understand gender relations beyond the masculine anxieties of Picasso as visible in *Les Demoiselles*. The most remarkable project in this regard came after the First World War, but was founded on vocabulary he had already developed soon after his arrival in Paris in 1904. In 1934 Brâncuși received a request from the National League of Women from Gorj, his native region, to build a monument to the heroes from that region of Romania who fell during the Great War, to be located in Tîrgu Jiu, a city close to his birth village.

In developing the concept for the three-part ensemble, Brâncuși reached back to the work he had commenced in 1909. The roughly 100-foot-tall first piece is the *Endless Column*,[44] composed of eighteen segments in a pyramidal shape (Brâncuși called them "beads"),[45] which he had used in several works for over two decades, including several smaller versions of the *Column*.[46] According to Brâncuși, the *Column* was a "stairway to heaven," a take on the biblical Jacob's ladder.[47] It was supposed to represent the visible link between the living and the dead, between the heroic self-sacrifice of the soldiers and the grateful remembrance of the living, as the original name of the piece suggested—*The Column of Endless Gratitude*.[48] Though in essence a phallic sculpture, this piece is not concerned with bringing homage to masculine prowess or virtue, but rather with the possibility of communicating with the dearly departed. It connects two worlds and renders the heavens accessible.

The second element, *The Gate of the Kiss*, uses the same visual representation of love as Brâncuși's earlier *Kiss*:[49] a circle comprising of two halves, held together through the geometric wholeness of that pure form. The gate is a place of transition and transcendence. To go through it is an invitation to reconsider oneself as the half of a whole. It also points toward a vision of gender roles that emphasizes partnership, equality, and complementarity, rather than difference and hierarchy.

Finally, passing through the gate one enters an alley flanked by seats and tall trees towering over the path, leading to *the Table of Silence*, a large, circular stone table with twelve seats around it. They are all executed in the same half-sphere, balanced gracefully on top of another half-sphere, echoing the theme from the *Gate of the Kiss* of the two halves as a whole. The *Table* is a place of reflection and acceptance of the sacrifice made during the war. It is also a place where everyone can sit down together as equal participants in enacting the process of remembering, thanking, and remaking life. Gender inclusiveness is implicit in this component, because of the use of the circle as union between man and woman from the *Gate* that precedes the *Table*.

Brâncuși selected abstract symbols of sacrifice, heroism, mourning, love, and memory as a means to connect all the living with the memory of the war dead, and to open up comforting interpretive possibilities for all visitors to the monument. His symbology, while anchored in Christianity, opened other avenues for interpretation on the part of any viewer through the minimalist visual vocabulary, as suggested by the multiple and competing interpretations on the part of generations of art critics.[50] By doing so, Brâncuși did not ignore gender. On the contrary, he offered new means for representing, identifying with, and critiquing gender norms. Though not a feminist, Brâncuși was a more generous and playful spirit than many of his contemporaries when it came to his engagement with gendered themes.

While Brâncuși, Picasso, and other Parisian artists were developing new visual language for representing gendered themes, with greater levels of abstraction and interest in expressing psychological processes, Gertrude Stein was becoming a powerful presence in these circles, making her own indelible mark on the ideas and aesthetics of modernism. Stein intensely cultivated a number of prominent artists of the day, most importantly Picasso, and also engaged in her own acts of creation, from fashioning herself and her household into a nursery of modernism (in the botanical sense), to producing literary works that pushed the limits of language in the same direction as cubists pushed the limits of the line and color.[51]

Her first published piece, *Three Lives* (1909), introduced themes and suggested the hermetic[52] style of writing she later became known for.[53] The three portraits represent attempts to work out unhappy love affairs Stein had wrestled with before moving to Paris. For instance, "The Good Anna" explores the power relations between the restrained and hard-working Anna and Mrs Lehntman, repeatedly identified as "the romance of Anna's life." Though short on any erotic explicit references, Stein's writing is more interested in the psychological dimensions of this subdued lesbian love, especially the frailty of bonds between one who wants another and the other who only needs, but does not necessarily want the one offering her love. Stein shows marriage as the only way to prevent the object of one's love from escaping.

The theme of the novella was new and is considered pioneering in the lesbian love story genre. There is also a novel type of wicked irony in relation to depicting gender roles, best expressed in Anna's relations with her dogs and in Stein's portraiture of the dogs' adventures. Finally, the story about Melanchta broke new ground in terms of imagining gender norms by offering a complex portrait of this heroine of color, a woman with a rich intellectual interior life, who develops intimate relations with men, and at one point with a woman, in search of erotic self-fulfillment. In addition to these thematic innovations, *Three Lives* also features some of Stein's repetitive style, her grammatical playfulness, and her relentless probing of the psychological states through jarring juxtapositions.

For all her innovation, Stein was still anchored in many of the assumptions about gender roles that framed her upbringing, and she remained so even as she became more famous and accepted in terms of her unconventional lifestyle. *Three Lives* describes lesbian love as friendship, the absence of passion and physicality in the portraiture rendering it less scandalous than it may have been otherwise. The power relations described in the novellas are also unequal, and the gender norms represented through them quite conventional. In fact, the persona Stein imagined for herself and performed publicly in relation to her lover, Alice B. Toklas, cast Stein herself as the powerful masculine genius of the couple, with Toklas as the "seen but not heard" feminine of the couple.[54] At the gatherings held in their famous apartment in Paris, Stein smoked cigars and discussed the avant-garde with the men in attendance at her soirees, while Toklas would escort the women to another room.

As a collector, host, and curator of modernist art, Stein played an essential role in framing the modernist canon (more on that in Chapter 3). Having carved out an exceptional niche for herself, she used her role of host to promote the work of geniuses that she viewed as her peers. That the world of art criticism only identified men as geniuses at that time does not seem to have bothered Stein. In fact, evidence from her private correspondence indicates that, in constructing an understanding of her gendered self, Stein took inspiration from the sexology theories of that time, especially the theory that identified superior intellectual capabilities (i.e., genius) with masculinity.[55] In the polarized view espoused by this new science, lesbianism was an inversion of women's normal gender identity, a form for masculinization. Stein chose to interpret these restrictive gender roles as a solution for her own internal struggle with who she was, and to see herself as indeed a male genius in a female body. By doing so, she nourished the legend of her own intellectual exceptionalism, reinforcing both intellectually and through her behavior, the restrictive roles for women that most modernists at that time were still unwilling to challenge.

The consecration of modernism as a major global movement came in 1913 with the Armory Show hosted in New York City in February–March.[56] The choices of the curators, the response of the critics, and the overall public reception provide important insights into what modernism came to mean just before the outbreak of the First World War. Organized by a relatively new network of artists, this exhibit familiarized the American public with a score of artists who later became part of the modernist canon, from Vasily Kandinsky to Marcel Duchamp, from Marie Laurencin to Picasso. The organizers differed over the criteria for selection and in terms of their own aesthetic sensibilities. Some were more favorably disposed than others toward the experimental newest forms, especially cubism and fauvism.[57]

Though the organizers did not express a feminist agenda, the show exhibited work by fifty women artists (out of around 300). In the final list, around 10 percent of paintings, sculptures, and other graphic and textile works displayed at the Armory Show were by women.[58] How these women were selected and how their work was exhibited tell us a great deal about the relationship between modernism and gender circa 1913.

One of the main co-organizers, Robert Henri, is a particularly illustrative example of this complicated relationship. Considered a main force for the modernist and anarchist movements in the United States, Henri lived in intimate proximity with women artists and feminists of various degrees of radicalness.[59] Emma Goldman was a supporter of his work, and he was married to a painter. He taught at a women's art school and understood first-hand the limitations of the established art academies in terms of women's access to art education. Yet Henri also stated: "An artist must be a man first. He must stand on his own feet, see with his own eyes, the brave eyes of bold manhood and report his findings in the straightforward unfinicky manner of the male."[60] This unabashedly masculinist statement shows that Henri harbored a derogatory view of women artists as lacking autonomy, derivative in their style, and missing the courage of direct and powerful plasticity that only men supposedly possessed.

Still, some scholars have acknowledged the significance of Henri as a teacher and mentor to women artists.[61] Comparing the work of Henri's female students to their male Ashcan School contemporaries, Marian Wardle asserts: "An examination of their experiments in many media illuminates a much broader application of Henri's modernist ideals. . . . Henri's women students contributed significantly to the structure of American modernism. They produced a large body of work, exhibited widely, won major art awards, belonged to and administered arts organizations, and taught art classes across America."[62]

Of the fifty women artists Henri helped bring into the Armory Show, almost half were or had been his students, or acquaintances that followed his school.[63] So it may be that he saw his own school as a superior brand of teaching women to become creative painters. Henri knew other women who were chosen to exhibit at the Armory Show through male artists, some of whom had yielded part of their own exhibition space to their female partners.[64] Finally, Henri had selected some women artists on trips to Europe. In a sort of affirmative action process, Henri picked a larger percentage of women out of the total number who applied as unsolicited artists than the percentage of men applying, even though more women overall applied directly. His anarcho-individualism prevailed in Henri's decision to embrace the greater diversity of artistic approaches offered by the presence of women artists in the exhibit.

* * *

The early decades of modernist experimentation saw the rise of both modest and radical challenges to gender norms in artistic and intellectual discourses. Most of these innovators were less interested in challenging gender norms than in engaging in aesthetic experimentation where gender and sexuality were a site of critiquing tradition, rather than the main focus of their work. Still, the artifacts they produced articulated new vocabularies that often implicitly and sometimes explicitly challenged the gender norms of that period. The multiplication of these new forms of representing masculinity and femininity broadened the spectrum of how both artists and activists would subsequently choose to engage more directly with gender.

2

Modernism Flourishes

The Great War

The coming of the First World War threw European societies into turmoil. In 1914, all the rebellions and all the utopias and dystopias imagined by writers, artists, and thinkers over the past decade were overtaken by unprecedented violence, from Moscow to Paris. The war upended stability in European societies and threw states, gender relations, morality, and the general sense of optimism that dominated the summer of 1914 into complete disarray.[1] As soon as mobilization went into effect, families found themselves struggling with basic economic needs, and women had to seek new roles in the home and in public arenas. In parts of Europe, women's entry into heavy industrial work was welcomed or at least viewed as a necessary means to enable economic production for the war effort and civilian needs to continue.[2] In other places, women were left to fend for themselves, unwelcomed in industrial production, unable to control the property of their husbands gone to war, and on the verge of starving their families without any legal and practical means to make money.[3]

As the war continued year after year, combatant states realized that they had been woefully unprepared for the destruction and paralysis that came to dominate many sectors of both civilian economy and the war effort. Women began to make do with the networks they created for food production and exchange, though such networks did not prevent bread riots from taking place on occasion, as the distribution of food supplies was not particularly well coordinated in both large cities and small towns. In Russia, for instance, the women's bread riots initiated some of the first widespread demonstrations in 1917, which grew into the Bolshevik uprising from February onward.[4]

In areas under occupation, such as Belgium and Romania, women also had to deal with a foreign army stationed in their neighborhoods and sometimes homes. Their lives depended on these armies, both literally and in terms of the availability of any services and jobs these women needed to keep their families alive. Some ended up working for the occupying armies, and after the war paid dearly for these choices, being exposed vociferously as "traitors" and "whores," often without any other evidence than the very fact they had worked as a secretary or domestic servant for a Central Power officer.[5]

As women learned to make do without their husbands, fathers, brothers, and sons, they also had to make do with the knowledge of the massive death toll on the front and due to the epidemics sweeping parts of Europe during and because of the war. This reality led many women to volunteer for the war effort in any capacity they were allowed to. Some volunteered directly on the front, taking on leadership roles through their ability to inspire others on the battlefield. Flora Sandes is probably the most famous of these volunteers, though she was by no means alone.[6] Romanians celebrate Ecaterina Teodoroiu as their Joan of Arc. Teodoroiu volunteered after her brother was killed and fought with bravery, being injured twice before she was killed during an attack in September 1917.[7] Russia had the only-female battalions, the most famous led by Maria Bochkareva.[8] These women were deemed exceptional both during their service and also after the war, and their personal example did not lead to different thinking about women in the military. In most cases, these women did not receive the same recognition and respect for their sacrifices (e.g., the title and benefits of being war veterans) as male veterans did. Still, their activities were both evidence of a modernist spirit in the realm of women's public roles and an inspiration for future generations of modernist innovators in matters of gender norms.

Women were more warmly welcomed as volunteers for the Red Cross and other organizations that aimed to provide a variety of types of caretaking for the military personnel, and at times for civilians as well. As Red Cross volunteers, thousands of women in all combatant countries placed themselves in positions of danger or at the very least in great discomfort. Some accompanied male doctors who served as officers on medical trains that operated in the same areas where heavy artillery fire took place. These women placed their lives in danger every moment they were there. Others worked in hospitals set up in many spots behind the immediate fighting front and confronted serious danger due to the moving armies (for instance, in Poland, Romania, or Serbia). Some women volunteers drove ambulances to and from the front, exposing themselves to aerial attacks by enemy troops.

Red Cross volunteers provided both medical and psychological support for the traumatized soldiers they came in contact with. The soldiers they took care of left behind descriptions that confirm that the presence and actions of these women kept hope alive among many of the wounded and offered comfort to those who died.[9] These volunteers also helped the prisoners of war, enabling them to communicate with their families as well as be taken care of by women whose nationalistic sentiments took a back seat to their humanitarianism.

While many women volunteered initially because of a sense of familial or national duty, wartime experiences turned some of them away from fighting for nationalism and toward supporting humanitarianism or pacifism. Vera Brittain volunteered to serve her country out of duty and loyalty to her fiancé, brother, and other male friends who served on the front. Slowly, she lost all of these beloved companions during the war. With the unfolding of the war, Brittain's nationalism turned into pacifism, and her literary career, which took off after the war, was dedicated to the cause of peace as well as to the cause of women's political and social equality with men. The rawness and intensity of her autobiographical writings about the war experience made Brittain an important force of inspiration for other modernist writers, among them Virginia Woolf.[10]

The Great War threw men's lives into great turmoil as well. Soldiering had long been an exclusive responsibility of men and, with the rise of the modern national state, the duty of every able-bodied adult male. Though all men were aware of these expectations, no soldier was prepared for the duration and intensity of the war as it unfolded. The cruelty they experienced and were forced to wreak upon others traumatized many soldiers. The nature of the trench warfare, its idle absurdity, and massive casualties that fouled the air for days before the bodies could be buried, pushed some of these young men over the edge, into insanity.[11] The British poet Siegfried Sassoon lost his grip on reality after participating in the Battle of the Somme, where a million men lost their lives for a few feet of soil. His wartime poems became both an indictment of the insanity of war and some of the most introspective modernist literature produced in the aftermath of this massive tragedy:

> Does it matter?—losing your legs? . . .
> For people will always be kind,
> And you need not show that you mind
> When the others come in after hunting
> To gobble their muffins and eggs.
>
> . . .
>
> Do they matter?—those dreams from the pit? . . .
> You can drink and forget and be glad,
> And people will not say that you're mad;
> For they'll know you've fought for your country
> And no one will worry a bit.[12]

Sasoon's poems expressed what millions of other soldiers experienced during and after their time in combat. Their trauma could not be understood by anyone who had not lived through those moments, and many came back with wounds that never healed. If women's roles in society were tested by the experiences of living in fear, poverty, and without news from their husbands and sons, masculinity was radically changed by the front.

Heroism, virtue, and courage were redefined through the brutality and inhumanity of the battleground. A soldier's nationality, skin color, religion, sexual preferences, or even rank were rendered less relevant in bringing meaning to their sacrifice on the battlefield than the sheer numbers in which these young men died. The most impressive monuments raised to these heroes after the war featured only their names, leaving unspoken any other information about any of them and equalizing their sacrifice across all other divisions: heroism was to lay one's life on the battlefield.[13]

At the same time, the number of people killed by friendly fire brought into question the notion of heroic self-sacrifice and shed light on the tragic aspects of the fighting. There were unprecedented numbers of men who fled from the carnage; the question of whether their actions were treason or could be viewed as justified under those horrendous conditions remained open long into the interwar period.[14]

Finally, as women volunteered and sacrificed their lives or health in the service of the same war, they confronted and challenged the masculinist assumptions about wartime heroism. Their actions were probably the most radical of all the unprecedented aspects of the war, and the reaction of the military and political leadership after the war suggests that European society was not yet prepared to shift expectations about gender roles this far: overall, war widows received greater public recognition and support (pensions) than women war veterans, many of whom were never given any public recognition, much less support for their sacrifices.[15]

In short, in the aftermath of the horrendous losses and mistakes made in the Great War, in most combatant countries the military establishment changed very little regarding women's presence even in the auxiliary forces. In addition, few modifications were made in the area of medical care and coordination with the military, where the lack of preparedness had cost the combatants millions of lives lost to cholera, influenza, malaria, and other communicable diseases, in addition to the untreated war wounds. This reluctance to address huge problems by loosening restrictions against women as participants speaks volumes about the limited willingness of the politically powerful to reconsider gender norms in all aspects of public life. Some modernist artists and writers responded strongly to these issues, as will be shown below. Others were uninterested or unwilling to engage them.

In addition to the unprecedented ravages, human and material, European political ideologies were also radically transformed by the experience of the war, and with them, European societies and eventually gender norms. Communism moved from a small coterie of radical thinkers and writers to become a mass movement in several European countries, from Russia to Germany and

Hungary, with wide consequences for the rest of the twentieth century. The Zionist movement developed new levels of radicalism and engagement with the Palestinian homeland after the peace treaties. Nationalism itself became radicalized in the form of exclusivist, most often anti-Semitic movements. Fascism developed out of the radicalization of socialists and nationalists in Italy during the war, and grew in popularity due to the discontentment and unmet expectations of political leaders and intellectuals. Feminism also developed into a more persistent presence all over Europe, in large part due to women's increased participation in many public roles and their frustration with the state's disregard for their rights and duties as citizens. Finally, pacifism grew as a reaction to the war, as a loose network of activists and artists. Many of the leaders of such networks were prominent feminists like Jane Addams and Rozsa Schwimmer.

Many of these political movements had modernist elements and counted among their fervent supporters artists and writers who self-identified as modernist. In fact, one important element of modernism after the First World War was the extent to which the aestheticist posture of modernists like Oscar Wilde was overtaken by politically engaged modernist artistic trends, from surrealism to expressionism. The war forced a breach in the sensibilities of most producers of culture, and in many cases contributed to their politicization.[16]

It is remarkable that all of these movements included women among their leaders and questions about gender norms at the core of their articulation of what was wrong with Europe at that time, as well as their ideas for change. The experience of the war, simply put, emboldened women toward asserting full agency in their societies.[17] Given the general trend of these radicalized ideologies to reject many of the principles and platforms of the existing parties, frustrated and emboldened women found promising avenues for empowerment in the new flavors of politics that rose out of the war, from democratic to authoritarian, from left-wing to right-wing. Some of them also found a sympathetic ear among men. I will return to this important development in Chapter 4, but it is important to keep this context in mind while exploring the new modernist trends in art and literature through the years of the war and into the early 1920s.

Dada

Among the new modernist groups that rose in the wake of the war, Dada in particular became identified with the rejection of the war—its motivations, goals, and overall participating in combat. With most European capitals engulfed in the war effort, after 1914 Zurich became an oasis of neutrality, where a number of artists and activists found refuge. Not only was Vladimir

Ilych Lenin around there in early 1916, but a number of art rebels, from the Romanian Tristan Tzara to the German Hugo Ball, came together at the Cabaret Voltaire club to work through the political and artistic questions that animated this proto-anarchist movement.[18]

The Dada movement was pointedly antiestablishment, and from the beginning welcomed men and women as partners in the happenings and activism of the group. The sensibilities of many male contributors veered toward nonsense anti-art, from Tzara's poems to Fracis Picabia's technical drawings. By contrast, women Dadaists took on a more constructivist perspective on their rejection of the establishment. Sophie Tauber-Arp produced a number of *Dada Heads* that showed primitivist influences, while being fashioned as potentially useful objects. One critic identified her style as "a feminine nuance of the Dada game: nonsense with a utilitarian purpose."[19] In the words of this critic, modernism was compatible with utility, and the feminine was about functionality. I would take the statement further and suggest that an important element women added to this movement was precisely to anchor their art in the social and relational, linking the artist to the public on several levels: the public was more than a viewer, becoming a user or participant in the unfolding of the event and consumption of the art object. The practical usefulness of such art objects lent them a familiar and intimate edge, that one often does not perceive in the more hermetic objects and texts generated by male Dada artists.

Another important woman artist in the Dada circles was Hannah Höch, who became active in connection with the Berlin group during and after the war. An accomplished graphic designer who made her living in publishing, in 1918 Höch discovered collages of photographs depicting German soldiers in several private homes. This representation of wartime suffering inspired her and led Höch to develop photomontage as a new and important modernist art technique, which inherently questioned the relationship between artist and creativity, placing technology and mechanization at the center of new ways of thinking about beauty. Höch's work both deconstructed reality as imagined or depicted by others through photography (she cut heads off bodies, parts of faces, etc.), and also refashioned power and especially gender relations through the juxtaposition of elements or body parts that did not fit together in any "normal," or rather expected fashion. While Höch was not alone in taking up this technique, her sense of humor lent itself to a satirical approach that was both direct and light, while keeping forceful feminist undertones.

Höch's best-known work, *Cut with the Dada Kitchen Knife through the Last Weimar Beer-Belly Cultural Epoch in Germany* (1918–19), is an incisive and humorous take on gender norms in late-imperial Germany from a resolutely feminist perspective. Höch created the piece as Germany was unraveling

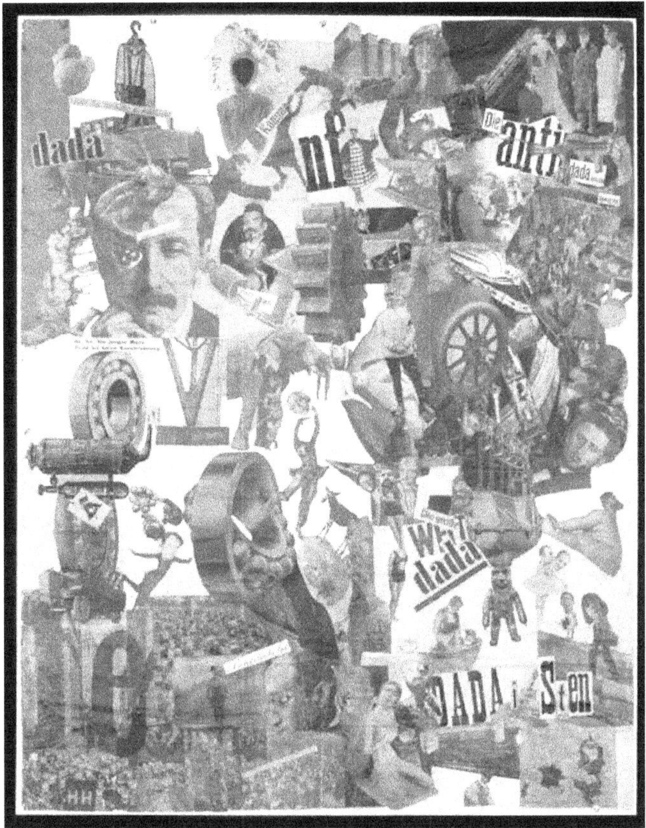

FIGURE 3 *Hannah Höch (1889–1978)*, Cut with the Dada Kitchen Knife through the Last Weimar Beer-Belly Cultural Epoch in Germany. *1919. Collage, 114 × 90 cm. NG 57/61. Photo Jörg P. Anders. Nationalgalerie. © ARS, NY.*

under the internal tensions generated by Central Powers' loss in the war and by the radicalization of left-wing and right-wing movements inside the country. In the center of the montage, a headless ballerina gracefully bounces a head like a beach ball, an image that communicates with dry wit the artist's view of women's roles in German society—objectified as pretty things, with no regard for or interest in what their minds have to offer. A similar jarring representation of the lack of regard for women's minds and interests appears toward the top of the painting, where she places the photograph of a cabaret dancer with the face cut out. Severe male figures look over this objectification of women, some of them prominent German wartime leaders in military garb, a reminder of the bleak events of the war. They are identified as "anti-Dada." By contrast, the heads of the communist leaders Lenin, Karl Marx, and Karl Radek bob above the text *"Die grosse dada"* (the great Dada).

Höch's work is both a strong statement about the politics and society of late-imperial Germany and a commentary on the ideological sympathies of the Dada movement. Her own view of these sympathies is not clear, however. The disembodied heads of these three communist leaders might suggest that their ideas have little to do with the reality on the ground. One could interpret the images to suggest that the artist considered only some of their ideas, rather than communist ideology in general taken at face value, as important or worth supporting.

Entwined with these political figures are gender-bending bodies, people featured in a combined male-female body, and in one case as a female ballerina body with two male heads. Höch lays before us dozens of such jumbled figures, like a queer sideshow of humanity that invites the viewer to step in and make sense of these images in our own way. She simply holds a funhouse mirror to the world created by the Great War. The carnivalesque humorous aspects of the montage notwithstanding, *Cut with a Dada Kitchen Knife* is a work of unmistakable feminist sensibility from the very title, offering a brilliantly original critical view of contemporary gender regimes and specifically power relations.

Höch and Tauber-Arp remained on the edges of the Dada movement. The men in the Dada circles happily used their female collaborators to stage happenings, put on cabaret shows, produce magazines, and sustain the daily working of these groups. Sometimes, these women artists, Höch among them, took on paid work to financially support their more famous male partners, putting their own creative process on the backburner.[20] However, when it came to Dadaist rejection of existing structures and values, traditional gender roles did not make the list of themes to be ridiculed in the performances staged by the men of Dada. Höch's call for women's suffrage found no echo in the work and happenings of her male colleagues. When major exhibits featuring Dada art opened after the war, contributions by women artists were left out or featured around the margins of these shows, and the movement presented itself as very much a coterie of male rebels. As the Dadaist leaders Tzara, Man Ray, and Picabia took residence in Paris and began new affiliations with André Breton and others to found the surrealist movement, they did not promote or support the work of their Dada female colleagues.

The contributions by women artists to the Dada aesthetic vocabulary and ideas remained buried for many decades, and are still being "discovered" a hundred years later. Höch had her first personal show in 2007.[21] In a major Dada retrospective hosted in Europe and North America in 2006, Höch was made visible through her *Cut with a Dada Kitchen Knife* and a few other pieces, but not as the central innovator she was. Her work appeared alongside that of Otto Dix, in essence as one among many. No reference to the gender politics and innovative contributions of Höch herself in this area appeared in the catalogue or aural commentary.

Even Max Ernst's expansive piece, *At the Rendez-Vous of Friends* (1922), featured as a sort of bookend to the 2006 Dada exhibit, received no gendered reading of its "family portrait" of Dada. The large canvas depicts a group of people whom the painter placed together playfully, to indicate both whom he viewed as important early influences for the movement (Dostoyevsky and Raphael) and the "movers and shakers" of the Dada movement, from André Breton (caped in red) to Jean Arp and Ernst himself. The sole female figure is Gala Eluard—not an artist, but the muse of several Parisian artists at that time.[22] She is also depicted at the outer edges of the group with her back turned toward the viewer, a mark of marginality.

By 1922, when the *Rendez-Vous* was completed, Höch had been showing with the Dada group for over two years alongside Ernst and other men depicted in the *Rendez-Vous*, inclusive of a major exhibition in Berlin in 1920. Ernst was familiar with her style and specific contributions. That he chose not to represent Höch in particular suggests he did not think much of her innovations and creative potential.[23] One might counter that many more prominent male than female Dada artists are absent from this group portrait. That is true, but the absence of any women artists from such a large and well-populated canvas that includes precursors and one marginal female figure suggests that Ernst simply did not regard women's creative potential and output significant enough to depict even one relevant representative figure.

Surrealism

Prefigured in the *Rendez-Vous*, the surrealist movement was the brainchild of Breton. Together with many Dada artists he attracted to his circle, Breton blended their nihilist message and new techniques, such as automatic writing, collage, and breakdown of perspective, to push the limits of artistic representation toward the irrational.

Breton's *First Manifesto of Surrealism* (1924), considered as the official crossover from Dada into surrealism, starts with an address to a particular category of readers: men.[24] Breton seemed interested in women predominantly as an object of desire or anxiety for men, rather than as an audience or participants in his experiment. Thus, even as he explored the irrational through language and engaged in exercises of reimagining the meaning of individual words and taxonomy, Breton never left behind traditional gender roles as framed through words. In his definition, "*homme*" (man) is not to be understood generically as "person." "Man," gendered masculine, is the quintessential dreamer, we learn from the second sentence of the *Manifesto*. He is defined in part by his knowledge of "how many women he has had."[25]

Whether a statement of fact regarding norms of masculinity in postwar France, or Breton's own interpretation of what the masculine irrational was driven by, the relationship of male subject to the female object became a leitmotif both in the *Manifesto* and subsequently in much of the work of writers, artists, and film makers affiliated with the surrealist movement.[26]

Breton was brilliant at cultivating a number of strong-minded artists of various genres around his surrealist grouping, and for the next decade he was the toast of Paris. In addition to many from the Dada movement, among the best-known artists of this group are Salvador Dali, Man Ray, Juan Miro, René Magritte, and Yves Tanguy. Desire mixed with sexual anxiety formed a dominant theme in the visual language of these artists.

A revealing case is presented by the twin images in the first (December 1924) and last (December 1929) issues, respectively, of *The Surrealist Revolution*. In the first issue, the surrealists dedicated a page to Germaine Berton, a famous anarchist who had been acquitted of murdering the secretary of the right-wing *Action Française* in 1923. Berton's mug shot, displayed as the largest image in the center of the page, was surrounded by headshots of famous artists either part of or admired by the surrealist movement, from Tzara to Picasso. Fearless and calm, Berton's eyes confront the viewer's gaze. At the bottom of the page, a quote from Charles Baudelaire provides the surrealists' commentary on Berton: "Woman is the being who projects the greatest shadow or the greatest light in our dreams."[27] In this iteration, the force Breton associates with femininity—the ability to cast light or shadow on the masculine irrational—becomes embodied in Berton's face and actions, as her image had become very familiar to the French public and immediately conjured up recollections of her violent actions and anarchist ideas. While evoking some anxiety, the collage overall appears celebratory of Berton's acts of violence against patriarchy of the nationalist Catholic kind, as embodied by the *Action Française*.

The last issue of *The Surrealist Revolution* offers a contrasting image of femininity, suggesting that the cry against the established order (and by extension patriarchy) was no longer a cause celèbre of the same magnitude. Entitled "Je ne vois pas la cachée dans la forêt " (I do not see the hidden woman in the forest),[28] the page is a collage comprising of headshots of prominent surrealists with their eyes shut surrounding a drawing by Magritte that depicts a nude woman looking away from the viewer in a pose that suggests both sexual provocation and modesty. The image grabs the viewer because of the stark contrast between the sixteen male heads in their suits, indifferent to the image at the center, and the vulnerable nude, one singular female figure drawn by a man's hand, and thus by definition the result of the artist's vision or desire. By contrast with Berton's piercing gaze, the anonymous nude woman looks down and away, shy or indifferent to the viewer. "Women" become "woman," an object of male desire and anxiety. In the surrealist universe depicted at the close of this publication, women were relegated to the role of objects, rarely possessing of characteristics that would give them an inner life. By exploring the subconscious and desire through the use of intensely gendered imagery, the surrealists focused almost exclusively on their understanding of masculinity in crisis, with women (or more often woman, as a generic type of symbolic figure) cast as a castrating, emasculating, and overpowering force they cannot escape.

The surrealists' commercial success has had important consequences for how we engage today with gender roles in modernist art. As modernism became big business starting a couple of decades ago, and as European capitals have started to rebrand for an ever-growing mass of tourists from all over the world, surrealism has emerged as one of the most popular aesthetics of the 1920s and 1930s. The work of Dali, for instance, has generated many derivative practices and products, from music videos to fashion. Even as

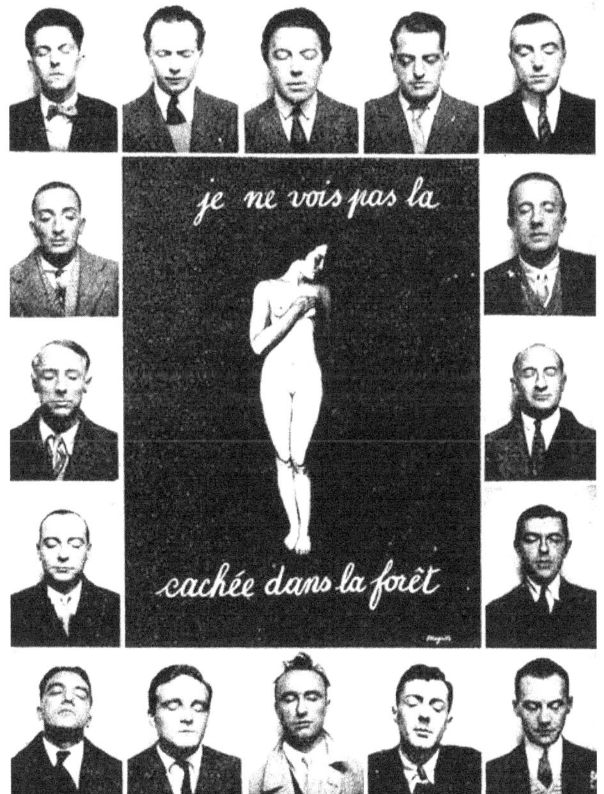

FIGURE 4 *"Je ne vois pas la cachée dans la forêt,"* La Révolution Surréaliste 5, *no. 12 (December 15, 1929): 73.*

generations of feminist critics have focused time and again on the misogyny present in surrealist art, museum curators have stayed away from any serious engagement with the gendered elements of the work of Magritte, Dali, Man Ray, and other luminaries of that movement.

And yet, one important exception needs to be pointed out: Frida Kahlo. Initially known internationally because of her association with her more famous painter husband, Diego Rivera, as well as other luminaries of the communist international networks of the 1930s, especially Leon Trotsky, Kahlo had her first solo shows in the United States and France, respectively, in 1938, through the patronage of André Breton. By the late 1930s, Breton was looking for a new generation of artists he could point to as the next wave of surrealists. Kahlo's intense canvases of dreamscapes, bodies, science drawings, and other jarring juxtaposed techniques, struck him as an extension of his own vision of surrealism.

Kahlo, however, did not set out to be a disciple of Breton, and while she agreed to the exhibits, it was on her own terms and for her own reasons. In the words of scholar Alice Gambrell, both Breton and Kahlo engaged in a sort of "Surrealist entrepreneurship."[29] If Breton's was an attempt to retain his primacy as the leader and original force of the surrealist movement, Kahlo used this attention to make internationally visible her unique vision of modernity, gender norms, motherhood, birthing, death, as well as many other themes present in her work, from race to mechanization. In the tense dance between these two egos, Breton asserted the voice of the narrator, depicting Kahlo as someone who was illustrating his own ideas through her vibrantly feminine (read intimate and emotional) style, which he saw as blending delicate beauty with a nervous disquiet about the female condition. He claimed that Kahlo painted in an innocent, naive manner, and defined her style as "spontaneous," as if "premeditated" would have taken something away from the quality of Kahlo's painting.[30] Though framed as a homage to a talented painter, the narrative Breton provided for the Kahlo catalogue suggested in subtle and not so subtle ways that she was neither an original nor a sophisticated painter, but rather an almost accidental disciple of surrealism.

Yet for the woman behind these canvases, her work and the publicity offered by the two personal exhibits were a vehicle for establishing exactly her originality and the complexity of her vision, from sources of inspiration to execution. As several studies have shown, Kahlo built her visual vocabulary as a mix of both traditional and modern, magical realism and literalness, juxtaposing intimate and mechanical elements.[31] She painted in direct relation and as a reaction to Picasso, de Chirico, and other modernist male painters who had appropriated female bodies to speak about the modern condition, with her own gendered take on the same themes of alienation, duplicity, and anxiety. But she used primarily her own body as the framework for articulating these issues, which led Breton and others to see her work as intimate and personal.

The continuous use of Magritte's wife's body, Georgette, never led his colleagues in the surrealist movement to regard him as sentimental, or too connected with his immediate emotional reality, neither did Man Ray's use of Lee Miller, his frequent muse and an original photographer with her own long and successful career as an artist. The bodies of these women were viewed as a raw material for constructing an aesthetic vision, rather than some confession of love. By contrast, Kahlo's equally obsessive use of her face and body were read at the time (and continue to be read today by many critics and viewers) as a type of unique egocentrism, of an emotional rawness that does not leave room for distance and irony. And yet, Gantrell and others show persuasively that Frida Kahlo used her biological self as a means to examine larger themes linked to the modern condition.[32] Her many self-portraits are as many masks, articulations of self-made identities that are never "spontaneous" or "natural."[33] By using her own body, Kahlo managed to transform the abstractly voyeuristic depiction of gender themes in surrealist painting into a forceful feminist deconstruction of gender norms without objectifying the female body.

Expressionism

The early years of the twentieth century, both before and especially after the start of the First World War, saw the flourishing of another important modernist art movement, expressionism, which had its most prolific followers in Germany in art, literature, and film. Like the French and Spanish surrealists, many German expressionists proclaimed themselves to be sympathizers of the left to various degrees of radicalness, and some supported the ideas of Marx and Liebknecht. Critiques of class inequality and capitalism were leitmotifs of much expressionist art and film. At the same time, most expressionists remained uninterested in a serious critique of patriarchy along the socialist lines offered by Friedrich Engels or Clara Zetkin (more of that in Chapter 4).

An illuminating example of this absence in the midst of a radical anticapitalist critique is Fritz Lang's science fiction film, *Metropolis* (1926). Technology, mechanization, and urbanization were important themes in modernist critiques of the establishment, and *Metropolis* used highly gendered images as metaphors for the perils of modernity and capitalism. The film depicts the rebellion of the working class against their oppressors in a futuristic society in which cyborgs walk among humans. Yet the aesthetics of the movie are more ambiguous and show both fear of technology and mechanization, as well as irrepressible attraction toward technological advancements, as many critiques have argued and viewers have demonstrated through the lasting impact of the film.[34] Lang chose to depict this ambivalent attitude by making a female character (and her sexualized cyborg double) the central vehicle of the film.

Maria, the human leader of the workers' rebellion, comes to represent the idea of betterment of humanity, albeit more abstract than physical. However, she is depicted more as muse rather than leader in the rebellion that ensues. In one critic's view, she represents the "heart" of the trinity of mind/body/heart that can save this polarized society.[35] Her cyborg double, by contrast, becomes the embodiment of both dystopia and daemonic irrepressible sensuality, but again as an irrational object or projection of a masculine mind, rather than as a willful rational actor. In these ambiguous representations of gender power relations and modern technology, *Metropolis* continues to use gendered symbols that do little to advance the cause of women's autonomy in contemporary society, and instead reimagine masculine anxieties related to women's empowerment and polarized gender roles as realities produced by technological innovation.

As film technology evolved to give rise to talkies, German filmmakers embraced these developments in movies like *The Blue Angel* (1930). Another modernist masterpiece, *Blue Angel* was based on an expressionist novel from 1905 by Heinrich Mann, which offered a wicked satire of bourgeois mores in late-Wilhelminian Germany. In the film adaptation, the satire is amplified through the unforgettable character of Lola-Lola, the first appearance in a spoken film by Marlene Dietrich. In Josef von Sternberg's interpretation, the film becomes a complex dance between the self-important and ultimately weak professor who seeks Lola's attentions, and Lola's own search for a voice on stage and in life. Emil Jannings, at that time a well-known silent-film actor, played Professor Rath with a compassion that brought ambiguity to the character, rendering him less of the cruel tyrant than the director had wanted to see.[36] In turn, Dietrich's portraiture of Lola is both frightening and compelling. Many have seen her character as a quintessential critique of the decline of the middle class and an expression of the male anxieties brought on by the appearance of the New Woman during the early decades of the twentieth century.

Yet the film provides a significantly more complex depiction of gender roles in this shifting environment, less arresting and more understanding than *Metropolis*, if only because of the nuanced and charismatic acting by the two main stars.[37] Dietrich's spellbinding performance as both cabaret artist and cross-dresser generated great numbers of both voyeuristic and admiring followers. Undoubtedly an emasculating character in her relationship with Professor Rath and thus reflecting the anxieties of many male viewers, Lola was also free, forceful, and unstoppable, and inspired many other women, artists or not, to self-identify with this emancipated New Woman.

Other German expressionist artists reflected on gender roles from an even more clearly feminist perspective, if with very different aesthetic and political preferences. Käthe Kollwitz, in particular, focused much of her postwar work on critiquing the ravages of war and modern capitalism in the lives of women and children. A supporter of Germany's war effort at the beginning of 1914, Kollwitz lost her youngest son early in the war and became a resolute pacifist, and she remained a committed socialist into the interwar period. Kollwitz had become a celebrated artist in Germany already before the war, her work focusing on themes linked to her socialist sensibilities. But her experiences in the war hardened Kollwitz's critiques of the existing social and political order and brought about significant changes in her techniques as a result of her emotional struggle with the meaning of the violence and suffering rising around her. Empathy and a commitment to the poor and vulnerable were the foundations of Kollwitz's artistic vision and commentary since before 1914, but they were etched with harder lines in the lithographs she produced after the war.

More than any other well-regarded artist of her day in Weimar Germany, Kollwitz placed her talent and stature in the service of social justice, with a focus on critiquing gender inequality.[38] Her choice of genre (she gave up painting and sculpture for the sake of creating images that could be mass produced) arose from Kollwitz's goal to reach both rich and poor, rather than to sell her work to rich collectors.[39] Her series of lithographs about the First World War focused almost exclusively on the suffering of women rendered vulnerable during and after the war—widows, pregnant women, mothers of small children. Kollwitz's depiction of these war victims is both empathetic and harsh.

The Survivors (1923), which was mass produced as a poster, forces the viewer to peer into the heart of darkness in the eyes of the woman at the center of the image. Her impenetrable gaze speaks of death and loss and refuses to acknowledge heroism or self-sacrifice as positive aspects of the wartime violence. These survivors demand that we acknowledge, however, their presence, their pain, and the fundamental injustice their broken, forgotten lives represent in postwar society. In essence, Kollwitz's work states over and over again the need to place these survivors—women and children— at the heart of rebuilding the postwar order, echoing the demands of her contemporary Social Democratic fellow travelers about women's political and economic emancipation.

The Modernist Novel after 1918

The New Woman was at the heart of many literary depictions in the interwar period, some of them celebratory, others cautious. *La Garçonne* (1922) became one such famous novel, causing both great consternation among the social elites (Victor Margueritte was rescinded his Legion of Honor after the novel was published), as well as a huge following (the book sold

300,000 copies in the first of many issues).[40] The cause of discomfort for many, including some feminist activists, was the novel's explicit depiction of lesbian relations. The book portrayed its emancipated central character as a woman who finds freedom from narrow gender norms after her fiancé cheats on her. Emancipation becomes identified with bisexual exploration, rather than with other elements of gender inequality, from political to economic. Though criticized by both the left and the right, throughout the interwar period Margueritte continued to build plots and create strong and rebellious female characters that advocated for women's suffrage and access to birth control.

Virginia Woolf's *Orlando* (1928) engaged with the New Woman through a different set of characters and plot. As one of the few women who appear in most histories of modernism and who is an uncontested canonical figure of this movement, Woolf's work and life have been subject to many scholarly analyses. By the time she published *Orlando*, Woolf had written several works that showed an ironic distance and sometimes condescension toward the suffragists.[41] Yet it is clear that, both in her personal life and in her writing, Woolf was intensely interested in critically examining contemporary gender norms. Around the same time she wrote *Orlando*, Woolf also penned her paean to women's liberation, *A Room of One's Own* (1929).[42]

Of her huge body of work, *Orlando* is possibly the most radical attempt to both critique gender norms and also imagine a world in which gender and sexuality become more fluid and less rigidly polarized. Though sex is part of Orlando's world, Woolf developed her transgender character as androgynous, a shifting persona between the male and female poles while preserving her or his intellectual and emotional integrity. Both fantasy and comedy, *Orlando* is a playful exploration of possibilities not yet available to women in the 1920s, but rather a projection of feminist desires into the realm of dreams. If the surrealists were enamored of objectifying women as a force that emasculated male desires, Woolf invited her readers to imagine a more generous and vibrant world in which desire was defined and fulfilled by androgyny, rather than through the polarization of gender roles and shoring up of aggressive masculinity.

Another important theme in interwar novels was the relationship between violence and masculinity, especially in the aftermath of the horrendous experiences that young men faced between 1914 and 1918 (and until 1921 in the Civil War in Russia). Starting with works such as Henri Barbusse's *Under Fire* (1916), writing by men who fought in the First World War engaged with the trauma and unresolved frustrations they faced after they returned home.[43] Theirs was a crisis of identity broadly felt all over the continent and across ideological, class, religious, and other divides. For some, like Gabriele d'Annunzio and Adolf Hitler, their postwar writing encapsulated a desire for revenge and recapturing of masculine prowess in the aftermath of the war. Others, like Barbusse, Eric Maria Remarque, or Jaroslav Hašek, took the traumatic experience of the war as a starting point for critiquing traditional masculine norms in relation to nationalism and violent action.

In the case of Barbuse and Remarque, working through the absurdity and violence of the experience of the front resulted in a cry for peace and for rebelling against nationalism as both a cause and a result of the war. Revenge was not the answer for these two men who served in the war. Questioning the rationale for such violent actions was the lesson they took away, and which they wished to pass on to other returning soldiers or political leaders with bellicose ideas after 1918. Their ruminations on the war, *Under Fire* and *All Quiet on the Western Front* (1929), became influential both in the peace movement and in the literary world.

While Barbuse and Remarque were sorrowful and psychologically introspective in their exploration of trauma and masculinity, Hašek constructed a humorous depiction of the warfront experience through his *Good Soldier Švejk* (1923).[44] Published before most other novels on the First World War came out, *Švejk* was a satire that, much like Chaplin's movies, struck at the heart of the mores of the upper classes and bourgeoisie, and placed a foot soldier with little education and social status at the center of recollections of the war in which the author had served. Hašek's depiction of soldiers' experiences on the front becomes a merciless critique of the expectations European societies and states had of men at that time. His novel pokes fun at many traditional aspects of gender roles with the same gusto, but without a particular agenda having to do with masculine anxieties in relation to feminism or the new roles taken on by women during the war. Instead, Hašek depicted masculinist military heroism as nonsensical. Švejk's actions were always a series of blunders that may or may not get him in trouble, but they were a continuous stream of misinterpretations of orders, ideology, and propaganda generated by the corrupt and self-important upper-class men in the novel. Ultimately, Hašek tells us, survival in the absurd total war between 1914 and 1918 came down to avoidance and refusal to buy into and act according to those who preached self-sacrifice. There was no justification for laying down one's life for ideas and goals that did not serve the men fighting in it. In essence, to be a man meant getting out of the way of such lofty goals that did not serve Czech society at large.

The Tramp: Masculinity Reimagined

While anxieties about women's new roles in society and men's own place in the world after the traumatic experiences in the First World War abounded among the surrealists, Dadaists, and other fellow modernist travelers, many artists found other directions to critique the existing tropes about masculinity. One such remarkable figure is Charlie Chaplin, whose films were at the core of developing this quintessentially modernist art form in the early twentieth century.[45] Chaplin's Tramp is one of the iconic male characters in cinema over its entire history. With his series of films featuring the Tramp, Chaplin developed a rich and novel representation of "the little man," gendered masculine while reaching elements of universality. The Tramp became a film icon during the First World War, and was deployed in the early days of war mobilization in a propaganda short film made by Chaplin. Charlot, as the character became known throughout Europe, with Chaplin's exuberant and comical physicality and his loveable pranks, took both the United States and European film houses by storm.

Charlot embodied a new type of man, whose masculinity was no longer identified with a harsh virility or physical prowess. Nor was he a good-looking guy able to sweep women off their feet, like Rudolph Valentino's characters. In essence, Charlot was the first male superstar whose main characteristics were poverty, self-effacing humor, a scruffy demeanor and dress, shyness in relations with women, and a kindness toward children that was most closely identified with women's proper roles in society at that time. In *The Kid* (1921), Charlot assumed the role of primary caretaker of an infant orphan. His ideas of proper care were comical (for instance, the swinging papoose he comes up with at the start), yet endearing and effective. Charlot was kicked around by the authorities throughout this and other movies, but his ability to pick himself up and keep going with dignity and humor created a powerful new set of images about what men could become. Instead of avoiding the issue of powerlessness, Chaplin embraced it. Instead of suggesting violent reactions to the loss of control over one's life, as many men felt after the war and especially during the Great Depression, Chaplin offered humor and a turn toward other rewards in life besides money and power.

Chaplin's deep humanism and pacifism undergirded his approach to comedy and his depiction of masculinity across his career. In *Modern Times* (1936), another hugely popular and important film featuring Charlot, Chaplin took a stab at critiquing the robotization of work and factory production. With *Metropolis* playing in cinemas for a whole decade, expressionist images depicting the dehumanization of the work environment through a female character had become abundant. Yet Chaplin chose not to use gender polarization as a way to critique workers' oppression. Chaplin's female characters were never exceptionally or singularly cruel, by comparison with the male characters that accompany them, especially those representing the social elites. His women characters were sometimes fallen, lost, or powerless; but he never identified them as the sources of male anxiety and powerlessness. The machine that "eats up" Charlot in *Modern Times* is just a machine, rather than a female-looking creation of a male evil genius, as Lang depicted the crisis of masculinity in *Metropolis*.

Cabaret: Gender Transgressions

The postwar world was also transformed by the proliferation of cabaret culture, both through films and also in real life. Berlin, Zurich, and Paris had seen a flourishing of this performative art form already in the first decade of the century.[46] But the end of the First World War offered greater opportunities for the performers and generated greater interest on the part of the public to revel in the sexualized, escapist atmosphere of the cabaret. At the same time, postwar cabaret introduced important elements of artistic innovation and political critique. The surrealists and their cousins, the Dadaists, were the first to blend highbrow and lowbrow into one performance, using cabarets as inspiration for other types of artistic output, as well as a stage for their writing, painting, and the performance of new types of music and dance.[47] The cabaret was also the space where sexualized performances of gender roles and cross-dressing often spilled into the interactions between performers and clients. Sex work happened both on and off stage in these speakeasies, and both men and women indulged in crossing over.

During the 1920s, the explicitness of the sexualized performances and innuendos in cabarets rose to new levels. Soldiers' experience of the war included intense homosociality and erotic experimentation, all of which was inextricably connected to the demands made on these men by the states that sent them on the front.[48] Though custom and legislation rendered any public displays of alternative sexuality forbidden in many places, cabarets, as private clubs, invited playfulness in exactly this area, emboldening experimentation with gender and sexual roles. It was this particular emphasis on pushing the envelope, sexually speaking, that attracted patrons as well as certain artists interested in cross-dressing, bisexuality, and homosexuality.[49]

For some performers, such as Josephine Baker, the sexualization of cabaret culture became an opportunity for launching successful careers. With the arrival of jazz in Europe after African American United States troops brought the music to Paris and elsewhere during the war, a number of African American vaudeville productions became part of a transnational circuit of entertainers and cabarets that traveled regularly through European capitals. Baker arrived in Paris with the "The Black Review" in 1925 and took the Parisian public by storm.[50] She remained in Europe for the rest of her life, loyal to a fault to a public she saw as less racist than her native United States.[51] However, much like Dietrich's Lola, Baker walked a thin line between empowerment through her charismatic, spellbinding performances, and objectification as an iconic example of blackness understood as primitive, overly sexual, and available for hire.

Still, there is no doubt that for both Baker and for generations of performers that followed her, the persona she built on stage—sexualized, alluring, primitive, electric—was of her own making and represented an effort at defining herself as a modern dancer and emancipated woman. Baker did not reject traditional gender roles in her performances and life as much as she gave new meaning to feminine sensuality and to racialized definitions of gender identity: in essence, she owned her depiction as a primitive African and transformed that representation into the persona of a modern "Nefertiti" that captured the attention of the Parisian public, and worked her whole life to turn fixed clichés into dynamic performances whose very mobility defied any stable, static definitions.[52]

Modernist artistic experimentations in both old and new mediums continued through the rest of the interwar period, though further constrained in authoritarian states such as Germany and Italy. New legislation as well as violent actions undertaken by fascist paramilitary units made it more difficult to defy social norms. Some of the new aesthetic elements of various modernist

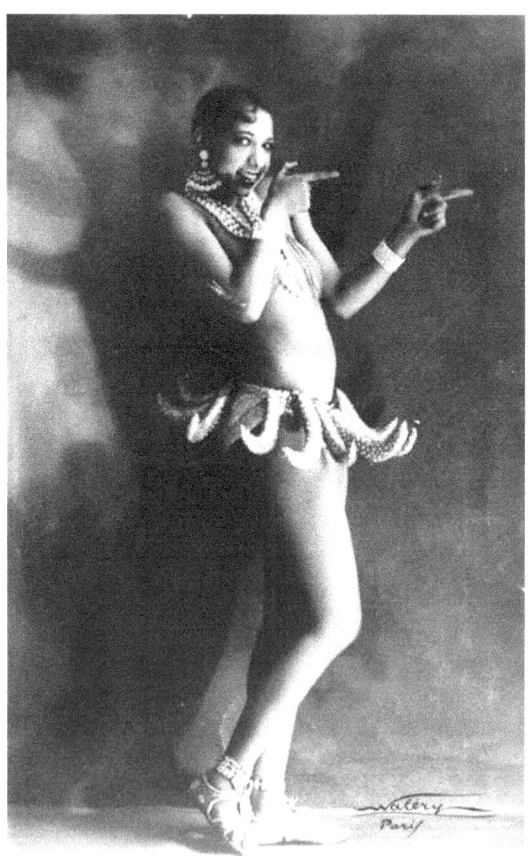

FIGURE 5 *Josephine Baker in the Banana Skirt, from the Folies Bergère production* Un Vent de Folie. *1927.*

movements were retained (e.g., the art deco clean lines in architectural design), but playfulness, inversion of norms, sexual explicitness, and any other deviations from naturalist representation became harder to incorporate in any form of public artistic work or performance. Paris, however, remained a haven for modernist writers and artists. Some also crossed the Atlantic to either return home or to escape the restrictions imposed by the Nazis in Germany.

The Spanish Civil War brought about a last spurt of modernist creativity before the whole continent descended into war again. It provided a framework for engaging in ideological struggle (communists, anarchists, fascists, and nationalists), as well as modernist experimentation. A significant number of modernist artists and writers joined both sides of the conflict, producing some of the most important and politically engaged artifacts of the entire modernist period. Picasso's *Guernica* (1937) became the most famous visual representation of that conflict, while George Orwell wrote one of his best-known works while fighting on the side of the republicans, *Homage to Catalonia* (1938).[53]

The Spanish Civil War offered unprecedented opportunities for women on the Republican side (i.e., anarchists and communists) to participate side by side with men in every aspect of preparation, propaganda, combat, and auxiliary support. Not every local leader promoted this type of gender equality, but the female volunteers who joined the Republican side were welcomed in many places. Some of them, like Dolores Ibarruri and Lina Odena, became well-known both among their fellow combatants and also among the international volunteers active in the war.[54] Others, like Gerda Taro, helped redefine photojournalism and the representation of war in the popular media, exposing its raw inhumanity in black and white. The significant presence of women in all these roles would not have been possible in Spain in 1937 without a shift in how supporters of the Republican cause, both women and men, imagined gender roles. The beginning of the Second World War, however, put an end to the age of experimentation as it had flourished in the arts and literature since the late nineteenth century. A very different political order and profoundly transformed societies emerged after that conflict, beyond the purview of this study. Modernism was itself reshaped by the radical global political realignments during the Cold War.

3

The Modernist Canon:
How Did it Come About?

The modernist works, individual representatives, and movements discussed thus far are part of a canon that started to be crafted during the period in which these innovators were active. To say that, in its formative period, this canon did not take questions about gender relations and norms as a core issue to be explored in terms of traditions and values the modernists rejected is nothing new. Critiques by artists and feminist activists at that time and later on by a variety of scholars have pointed out this issue over and over again.[1] Yet the canon survives until today with few changes in many literary anthologies, museums, and historical analyses of modernism. My analysis turns next toward the question of how this canon came into being and what are the implications of this process for understanding the relationship between gender and modernism.

Three elements converged to give the modernist canon its shape, and I will analyze each of them in terms of engaging gender norms: (1) the immediate context of how producers of culture chose the creative path for their artistic interest (e.g., education, publication, production outlets, or opportunities for public performances); (2) the economic dimensions of selling, collecting, publishing, and overall bringing into public view the works of individual producers of culture; and (3) the role of critics and scholars in reflecting on the canonization of specific individuals and movements self-identified with modernism. As my analysis shows, in all three areas important factors limited the opportunities for women to enter the world of the canonized modernists. The larger structural as well as specific discursive practices that dominated these areas of cultural activity also mitigated against significant challenges by feminist practitioners to question the masculinist assumptions about access to resources and public recognition. Simply put, those who questioned the implicit (and sometimes very explicit) misogyny of the cultural establishments found few established modernist figures to support these challenges. With the exception of very few who succeeded in pushing a feminist agenda under such unwelcoming circumstances, such as Virginia Woolf, most producers of culture with both a feminist and modernist agenda have remained at the margins of the canon. Because their work has not been integrated in broad analyses of the movement, our understanding of modernist challenges to gender roles is still relatively underdeveloped.

Schools, Academies, Guilds, and Journals

Artistic education, from painting and sculpture to theater directing and writing, was still the prerogative of men into the early decades of the twentieth century. Art academies in particular were extremely reluctant to abandon the double standard that had long anchored their exclusion of women from the ranks of students. Since the Renaissance, the painting of nude bodies had become an important component of training future artists.[2] As art schools became art academies with increasingly rigid rules about admission, the dilemma of whether women should be allowed to gaze upon a naked male body in public (i.e., in the art studio) was resolved by the male establishment in favor of the potential male students and to the exclusion of all female students: it would be inappropriate for women to study nude bodies, and thus women would have to be separated from men and guided toward the study of natural subjects or nonhuman bodies.

The absurdity of this exclusion is patently clear today and might have struck some people back in the post-Renaissance world in the same way. For the human being who is biologically shaped to give birth, and who presumably also engages in sexual relations with another human being as a matter of her wifely duties, how could it be inappropriate to look at and paint a naked human body of either gender? Yet such obvious issues were deemed inappropriate for discussion in any civilized public setting, and thus the exclusion of women from art academies became a norm, especially in the nineteenth century. Those inside such establishments had no interest in challenging women's exclusion, and women did not have an opportunity to push against these norms until the late nineteenth century.

The medieval guild system, which stood at the basis of early modern art academies, rarely accepted women among their members. The tradition of taking in young boys, training them through a live-in apprenticeship process that in essence rendered apprentices members of the artist's household, made it difficult for young girls to be accepted, because of the wider social norms and established practices regarding gender roles. Sometimes young daughters of artists were trained in the same way as young male apprentices, but such practices did not widen to include more women in most guilds.[3]

Attitudes toward women's education changed significantly between the Renaissance and the nineteenth century, but with little impact on the ways in which art academies and guilds operated. In response to the exclusivist policies of the best-established institutions of art training and professional organizations, more gender-enlightened benefactors opened up opportunities either exclusively for women or co-ed. Such opportunities developed quicker in places like the Netherlands, some German principalities, and England. But these newer enterprises were shunned by the established academies and guilds in other European countries, making it difficult for the work of women artists to be known in public.[4]

Starting in the late eighteenth century, important challenges to these norms began to take place in Great Britain and the Netherlands. The Royal Academy in London was established in 1768 by a group of artists that included two women. Angelica Kauffman was one of these pioneers, and she was also active in the Blue Stockings Society, which suggests that broader interests in enhancing women's participation in the arts and education animated her activities.[5] Yet after the death of these two women members, no other female artist was admitted to the Royal Academy until 1936, a good indication of how far the pendulum swung back against challenges to gender roles for over a century.

In France, until 1897 women were not allowed to sit in for the entrance exam at the National School for Fine Arts, established in 1816.[6] Women interested in pursuing art training had more options starting 1868, when Rodolphe Julian established a school that both trained artists for entry into the competitive National School and admitted women into their classes. However, in both that school and others that were co-ed, women often had to pay significantly higher tuition fees than men. Thus, for young men and women who wished to gain admission to formal art training, the bar was set at different heights, and various structural limitations along gender lines rendered such access much more restrictive for women as a category than for men: women had fewer opportunities to accumulate the necessary funds; they encountered legal restrictions in terms of using even financial resources they were entitled to; and in some countries women could not move to new places and reside there without the explicit permission of their fathers/husbands.[7]

It is thus not surprising that women sought different avenues for nurturing their passion for artistic creativity, sometimes via informal groupings and training, and increasingly through networks and institutions opened solely to women. These separate avenues afforded women greater access to education and exhibition spaces, since they were unlikely to be crowded out by their male counterparts in the same way they were at other more established Salons. However, by doing so they risked becoming less integrated overall in the conversations about what was new and exciting in the male-dominated art world. With the exception of those either already committed to supporting women artists' work or curious about this novelty, the new networks, schools, and exhibits opened exclusively to women did not attract sufficient attention on the part of the critics, wider public, collectors, or male artists to shake up the male art-world establishment.

When at the turn of the twentieth century, male artists such as Henri Matisse and other Fauves decided to break ranks with the art establishment as a means to push their ideas of change and rejection of tradition, they generally showed little interest in including female modernist artists among their ranks. Their struggle was against the academy and its strictures, but only on behalf of their own desire to be seen and appreciated. These modernists had the luxury of being able to say "no" to institutions that in principle allowed them to seek acceptance. Their revolt was against what they saw were limiting aesthetic horizons, rather than against wider forms of inequity or injustice. The extent of their rebelliousness and thus modernism needs to be understood in terms of the distance between, on the one hand, what these male artists had access to by virtue of their gender before their explicit revolt against tradition, and, on the other hand, the results of their rebellion.

It follows that women's rebelliousness as modernist artists should also be viewed in terms of the distance between what they could aspire to structurally before the time of the modernist rebellions, and the choices these women made to break ranks with those established traditions. And here is where their contemporary critics, their fellow male artists, and generations of scholars since then, have failed to properly measure the value of these women artists' work. If women had no access to the established art academies, Salons, and other institutionalized vehicles for becoming consecrated artists, they had to undergo a much longer route toward achieving recognition and becoming appreciated on their own terms. Their revolt was against invisibility and marginalization, and their aspirations focused on being taken seriously as professional artists.

An illustrative example is that of Romanian painter Cecilia Cuțescu-Stork. A talented and ambitious artist born into a family with long ties to the art world, Cuțescu-Stork traveled to Munich and Paris after exhausting the very limited avenues for art education available to a young female artist in her native Romania. During the 1900s many ambitious budding male artists from all over the world made the trek to Paris, the most successful enrolling in the Académie Julian. Robert Henri, for instance, studied at the Julian before returning to the United States to develop similar opportunities there.

For young women with the same artistic ambitions and passion for art, such opportunities were far more limited. Cuțescu-Stork was lucky in this regard: her family supported her aspirations and, instead of marrying her off, they spent considerable amounts of money to send her to Munich and Paris. Settling in Paris as an unmarried young female artist also carried risks for her, as Cuțescu-Stork's reputation and social standing back home could have been easily compromised through many types of unremarkable acts (real or rumored) of independence. But she was fortunate to avoid any such outcomes, primarily because of the wealth and discretion of her family. As she settled in Paris and began to exhibit, sometimes together with her friend and compatriot Brâncuși, Cuțescu-Stork carved out a good artistic reputation. Yet she left the Parisian scene behind because of an unhappy marriage and divorce.

Back in Bucharest, Cuțescu-Stork put her knowledge, financial support, and strong feminist convictions to work on behalf of starting a society for women artists and opening up more opportunities for women's access to art education.[8] As a promoter of modernist aesthetics and feminist leader, Cuțescu-Stork played a major role in reshaping the art world in Romania, inclusive of reimagining gender norms for women and public opinion about women as artists.[9] Yet she is little known outside of Romania today, and even there, she is considered primarily a "decorative" artist, while many more male artists from her generation have risen to greater prominence, even those who engaged in fewer modernist innovations.[10] Similar examples of extremely active, but forgotten women modernist artists with an interest in challenging gender roles with their words, actions, and visual representations, exist elsewhere in Eastern Europe, from Poland to Yugoslavia.[11]

As Cuțescu-Stork's brief biography indicates, the choices women had to make were often more costly and complex than the options available to men. Their struggles resembled, though were many times not part of or coordinated with, the feminist movements of the day. If women wanted to be heard and seen, they had a better chance of reaching a wider audience (as well as collectors) if they played up what was understood at the time as "feminine" aspects of their work, from genre (e.g., decorative arts) to subject (e.g., still life). But, playing up these elements made it particularly difficult to challenge the larger institutional contexts and gender norms that anchored such expectations.

If women wished to move away from such expectations and produce works that challenged gender norms, they stood little chance of a long-term career. Their options would be to "paint like a man" as a way of entering the male-dominated art movements of the day, or to move away from any association with either the male-dominated new modernist trends or with the feminine. The risks entailed in making either choice were great. The former option might depart from expectations regarding female artists, but it coded innovation in terms of masculinity, which again did not advance challenges against gendered assumptions about creativity. The latter entailed a life of toil and little chance of recognition. For instance, for someone like Hannah Höch, who very clearly shunned gendered expectations and developed a very original modernist style, the willingness to have the time to work on her collages and exhibit rested on her ability to support both herself and her male partner by working as a skilled wage earner. She had to take on the double burden of being both bread winner and creative spirit in her relationship with Raoul Haussman, who was also married to another woman at the time. Höch left Haussman when he insisted in turning this relationship into a ménage a trois, with Höch still cast in the supporting roles of bread winner and lover.

Women who wished to combine a family life and art career had notoriously difficult choices to make when these ambitions came in conflict because of their partners' expectations of what wives and mothers were to do in the household as their primary role in the relationship. For women who wished to live the bohemian unattached life of an artist, erotic relations in a period of unavailable birth control brought about other harsh choices men never faced. Marevna, a modernist painter who had a child with Diego Rivera during a short-lived relationship they entertained in the bohemian art world of Paris in 1912, wrote bitterly about gender inequities in the art world:

> My exhibitions were always followed by long blanks, because I had to fight fearfully to bring up my child, devote much time to commercial art. . . . All my life unfortunately, money has come between me and my work. In order to paint a woman must enjoy a certain security, even if she has only a quite small family to support. For the man the problem is easier to solve: he nearly always has a woman, wife or mistress, who earns money: she works for "her man."[12]

No male artist, writer, or producer of culture associated with the modernist canon had such a story to tell. None had to consider the stressful combined responsibilities of primary parenting at home, household caretaking overall, primary breadwinner, and cultivating one's passion for artistic creativity. The playing field was far more complicated and with greater and more complex obstacles to overcome for women interested in bringing innovation to aesthetic experiences and norms. Their courage and success in doing so can only be fully understood and appreciatively integrated in the history of modernism, broadly speaking, if we acknowledge the significant differences in terms of opportunities and traditions that separated women from men throughout this period.

If until the twentieth century, access to high-quality, formal art education proved difficult, if not impossible for women to achieve, it did not mean that women clamored to enter these establishments in droves afterward. Financial burdens, much higher for them than for men, created by the more expensive entrance and attendance fees and misogynist practices of admission and in the studios, continued to create an atmosphere in which women felt unwelcome. Many still chose to attend women's art academies for this reason, and others chose to attend other schools that were opening up with the flourishing of the arts and crafts movement around the same time.[13]

One of the important new avenues for women's art education and practice was the arts and crafts movement, associated with William Morris in Great Britain and with a number of different schools of design in continental Europe and North America. The impetus for these schools differed among their initiators, and some were more radical than others in their departure from traditional structure or organization, aesthetic orientation, and craft practices.[14] One important element related to the theme of this book is that these schools admitted women as students with greater ease than the art academies. At the same time, the curriculum in these schools included a great deal of traditional art training, as a means to enhance the design and production process in marrying functionality with beauty. Finally, some of these schools included what were considered up to then traditional women's decorative arts (e.g., knitting, embroidery) as integral aspects of interior and decorative design. In short, this became an avenue for young women of any social standing to gain substantial skills as an artist and to secure a job in an area that used these talents.

In Germany, artists like Höch honed their abilities to draw and design in such schools and managed to find employment afterward as a means to support both their own higher aspirations as independent modernist artists and sometimes their male partners with similar aspirations. In the United States, Tiffany's depended on women designers for their success in developing the stained glass artwork that became a signature for the brand: the Tiffany lamps.[15] The art nouveau movement, which concentrated so much on decoration, interior architecture, and design, grew to a significant extent because of the work done by the hands of thousands of women, mostly unknown until today, in areas that ranged from jewelry, ceramics, textile, and stained glass design, to the production of these functional objects.[16] These women were skilled and talented workers, but they were also artists, designers, and their sensibilities come through clearly in these functional objects of great beauty. The blend of organic and abstract that anchors the modernist aesthetic of these artifacts constitutes the original creation of those women designers, inclusive of their gendered sensibilities, their specific understanding of what a home is; what functionality meant for the mostly female users of these objects or managers of households; and how to push forward with new ideas in this area in which women were the main consumers and often buyers of the art objects.

Yet most consumers, art collectors, scholars, and more recently museum curators, did not know until very recently that many of the artists behind these exquisite art objects were women. It was only in 2006 that historians and curators at the New York Historical Society "discovered" Clara Driscoll as the artist behind the most celebrated Tiffany lamp designs from the turn of the century, such as the daffodils or the wisteria. From a modest social background, Driscoll was encouraged by her mother to pursue her interest in the arts and attended design schools in Cleveland and then New York City, where Tiffany hired her to work in the glass cutting studios. She worked there for over twenty years and moved up to become the director of the Women's Glass Cutting Department, making a salary that placed her at the top of her profession among peers.

Despite her gorgeous designs and the great success the studio achieved during her over two decades of working there, Driscoll was fired in 1909, for the simple reason that she chose to marry. Tiffany's only allowed unmarried women to work in the studios. In contrast, any man was free to apply for a job there and was never fired for making the same choice as Driscoll. As in many other workplaces at that time, misogynist assumptions about employment and economic responsibilities anchored the hiring and firing practices at Tiffany's, and Driscoll became a victim of these gender norms. Knowing that one of the most successful, talented, and prolific female designers was treated with so little appreciation and respect by the company to which she dedicated her professional career, one can only imagine what the work environment was like for any woman in this and other similar enterprises.[17]

Driscoll's story reveals significant structural impediments of a strictly gendered nature that women interested in pursuing an alternative art career faced. The legislation, cultural attitudes, institutional frameworks, and economic power were controlled by men who at best wished to use the talents of these women, but had no intention in treating women with the same respect and integrity with which they treated men. The success Driscoll and others like her achieved was bitter sweet, as it led neither to any recognition of women's talents overall, nor to any changes in the gender double standards in the practice of art studios and design workshops. It was only with the enfranchisement of women after 1918 that some of these tremendous structural gender inequities began to be eliminated, but it took decades and another strong wave of feminism in the 1960s before practice and cultural attitude caught up with women's own desire to have the same opportunities to pursue their love of art and design as men.

Other areas of intense experimentation and cultural production associated with modernism showed similar, though not as overt, forms of exclusion by the male establishment of women participants as full members. The publications started by some of the experimental writers associated with Dada or surrealism, for instance, were formed around one or several leading figures, all men, and the manifestoes as well as rosters of writers affiliated with these publications, such as *La Révolution Surréaliste* (see Figure 4, p. 41), made it clear that women existed as objects or inspiration for the movement, rather than as participants in shaping the ideas and aesthetics of these movements.

Until relatively recently, the scholarship on the literary periodicals that launched the career of many canonical modernist writers, from James Joyce to Mina Loy, focused on the leading male figures of these publications. *The Little Magazine: A History and a Bibliography* (1946) crafted a narrative that linked these activities to the development of modernism and articulated a strong argument for closely examining editorial power over shaping literary careers.[18] Yet this book showed disregard for the crucial work women had done in this area, to the point of distorting obvious facts.[19] More recently, a series of studies focusing on the impact of the "little magazines" on the crafting of the modernist canon have brought into sharper, critical, as well as appreciative focus the work of both men and women editors and their publications on critiquing established gender norms and providing outlets for experimentation with new ideas and aesthetic forms on the part of modernist producers of culture and activists.

A good example of the important work done by such journals is *The Little Review*. Founded by Margaret Anderson in Chicago (1914), the journal came out in monthly issues for six years, then in quarterly issues until 1929, when it ceased publication. The life of the periodical was complex, due to the personalities and aspirations of the editorial team.[20] But there is no question if both the vision and the will to publish the specific materials that came out in this journal, especially during its formative years, were grounded in Anderson's personal ideas about and taste in the arts, as well as her political interests, which encompassed both feminism and anarchism.

In early analyses of *The Little Review*, Anderson was depicted in derogatory terms as "quixotic," unfocused, lacking professionalism, and overall without a vision.[21] Yet, as recent scholarship has made it clear, this journal expressed the editor's desire for exposing a wide readership to the great variety of new ideas and aesthetic forms pouring out of every corner of North America and Europe.[22] That Anderson left part of an issue blank due to insufficiently interesting or provocative submissions also suggests that she was intentional, focused, and truly visionary in her editorial choices.[23]

In terms of speaking to gender norms, *The Little Review* played a significant role in publishing the work of more women modernists than virtually any other such journal. From Emma Goldman to Gertrude Stein, from Djuna Barnes to Elsa von Freytag-Lorinhoven, powerful female voices were present in the pages of the journal, exposing readers to the sizable diversity of innovative concepts and approaches to art and political activism these women brought to the debates of the day. *The Little Review*'s editorial vision and choices also show clear evidence of the unabashed feminist attitude Anderson espoused. In the first issue, she stated:

> [*The Little Review*'s] ambitious aim is to produce criticism . . . that shall be fresh and constructive, and intelligent from the artist's point of view. . . . Criticism that is creative—that is our high goal. And criticism is never a merely interpretive function: it is creation; it gives birth! . . . Feminism? A clear-thinking magazine can have only one attitude; the degree of ours is adamant.[24]

Materials that tackled gender norms from a critical feminist perspective were in fact a leitmotif of the journal while Anderson worked as its main editor. In the manner promised at the start, she opened the pages of *The Little Review* to a variety of feminist voices, as well as to strong critics of the suffrage movement, such as Emma Goldman. Anderson's goal, as suggested above, was to foster and widely disseminate creative, appreciative, and intellectually vigorous debates on sexism and women's movements, rather than advocacy from a single perspective. This spirit of curiosity and generosity as a host to so many different original voices in the debates over gender roles regarding ideology, aesthetics, religion, law, and other areas was Anderson's richest and most unique legacy to modernism.

The one genre of modernist cultural production where women did not face the same sort of sexist exclusionary practices regarding training and becoming visible was cabaret. With the female body, often naked, at the center of most cabaret scenes, women contributed significantly from the beginning to shaping the content, style, and production of these performances. Women were seldom in the position of producing or directing such performances, but the genre of cabaret lent itself to a collage of mini-productions, and for many performers, especially women, this structure provided greater freedom and visibility as the creative spirit behind the performance.

Emmy Hennings is a great example of a modernist artist who found her stride on stage. Hennings wrote poetry, performed as a puppeteer, and danced, finding an outlet for these talents at the famed Cabaret Simplicissimus in Munich. This is where she met Hugo Ball, with whom she moved to Switzerland at the beginning of the First World War to help found Cabaret Voltaire. Unlike Hennings, Ball is well known today for establishing the Dada movement at Cabaret Voltaire. But Hennings also played a core role in attracting attention to the performances at Voltaire, as observers at the time noted:

> The star of the cabaret however, is Mrs Emmy Hennings. The star of who knows how many nights and poems. Just as she stood before the billowing

yellow curtain of a Berlin cabaret, her arms rounded up over her hips, rich like a blooming bush, so today she is lending her body with an ever-brave front to the same songs, that body of hers which has since been ravaged little by pain.[25]

Ball himself acknowledged Hemmings as a partner, but other male members of this group relegated her activities as secondary to their writings, songs, and images.

One rare exception of a performer being able to control her image and garner recognition for her creativity as a primary artist is Josephine Baker, whose famed arrival to Paris has already been discussed in this book. An important aspect of Baker's artistry and the overall persona she cultivated on stage is the unique blend between ultra-modern and primitive she carefully shaped. After the First World War, with the spread of touring troupes through Europe featuring all-black casts, cabaret culture added an important race element especially in sexualized dance performances. Baker was not the first to appear nude or nearly nude on stage, performing dances that evoked an African exotic phantasy world for the voyeuristic white audiences. But she managed to move from an object of fascination (with her specific facial and bodily features, which for many represented the epitome of black female beauty) to become the force controlling her performances on stage. Baker "worked" her audiences in terms of their racist assumptions about beauty, sexuality, and modernity. She used her body to attract and challenge, manipulating the curiosity and discomfort of the white audiences in Europe to perform her own version of the New Woman.

Another dance revolutionary who managed to retain control over her persona and also succeeded in developing schools that brought her philosophy and techniques to future generations of women is Isadora Duncan. Duncan's insistence in eliminating the formal techniques and attires associated with classical ballet and insistence on privileging the natural shape of the body (and especially women's bodies) and free flowing movements represented a radical departure from dance performances at that time. Duncan thought of herself in terms of the ideas her dances communicated, as a philosopher and educator who worked through dance, rather than as a dancer who applied principles of movement to her performances.[26] In fact, Duncan relished teaching and working in the studio above public performances.

Considered an important formative figure for modern dance, Duncan created dance techniques, a visual aesthetic of the female body, and specific training and performance methods that profoundly challenged how women engaged as choreographers, educators, teachers, and spectators with gendered forms of beauty generated through the female body. Her schools, performances, and ideas, as communicated through a variety of mediums, placed women at the center of this process, as un-corseted (literally and figuratively) individuals, fully empowered to experience movement free of the academic constraints that preceded her.

I have been suggesting that avenues for women to pursue the arts changed significantly between the last decade of the nineteenth century and the First World War. This shift needs to be fully considered in our analysis of modernism and gender norms, for it shows important structural limitations that help explain why fewer women took part in the early period of modernist experimentation. The changes described here also help us better understand why and with what results many more women became active in this movement after the turn of the century. This larger context enables us to see how traditional gender norms were both limiting and eventually a target of modernist activism. The role played by women as the architects of their own empowerment demonstrates how modernism became both the process and outcome of a revolution in the arts. In this process, women used every opening and challenged sexist obstacles to redefine what modernity could become in the image of their own frustrations and aspirations.

Collecting

Collecting was a core component of articulating modernism and establishing the modernist canon. Thus, we cannot fully understand the relationship between modernism and gender without looking into the cultural, sociological, and economic aspects of the process of collecting. To begin with, the grouping of individuals around a term or movement self-identified as modernist was a trend that began with this period. The manifestoes produced by a variety of poets, artists, and other producers of culture aimed to define and limit the ideas and aesthetics affiliated with that specific movement, as well as the coterie of people who would be considered exemplars of that movement.

Thus, initially "collecting" meant the assemblage of artifacts and people around specific movements, and it started with the modernists themselves. The best-known and certainly most evocative example in terms of gender roles is Gertrude Stein. Stein defined herself as a modernist and profound innovator both through her writing and through the collection of people and works of art that she assembled in her Paris home.[27]

Stein began experiments in writing before she settled in Paris in 1903 in a home she shared with her brother Leo and his wife, Sarah. With a comfortable inheritance in hand, all three Steins became keenly interested in collecting art, though scholars differ on whose influence was most important than the other members of the family.[28] Their collective efforts had a profound and long-lasting impact on how the modernist canon came about. The tradition of patrician women hosting Salons for the artistic elites was very old, but what Gertrude Stein did with it profoundly shaped the face of modernism and many of its legacies.

Before she collected art, Stein collected people for her Salon. She quickly became famous for hosting excellent gatherings from food to the diversity and fame of those in attendance, and for being a demanding and quirky host herself. Stein took on a masculine cross-dressing persona to fit the developing sense of her queer self. She also made no secret that she preferred the company of the men she invited over, leaving it to Alice B. Toklas, her life partner, to both vet the female companions invited to the apartment and host those companions for tea and other feminine entertainments in a separate space, while Stein smoked cigars and talked modernist art with Picasso, Breton, or Man Ray.[29]

That is not to say that some women guests did not enjoy the same courtesy as men at Stein's soirees. Mary Cassatt was once invited, and a number of other female artists, writers, and art collectors, such as the Cone sisters, also graced Stein's home once in a while. But many of these women did not return for a second visit, sometimes because they resented the gender breakdown of these gatherings, and often because they simply disliked Stein's self-aggrandizing antiques and masculinized persona. Cassatt, for instance, lasted for just a brief visit with the potential collector and patron, and never returned.[30] Djuna Barnes also expressed disappointment at Stein's interest only in her looks, rather than her writing.

Unorthodox in many other ways, Stein shaped her Salon and art collection around her own ambitions as a writer, instigator of ideas, and genius of modernism. Her choice to self-identify with masculinity and to see genius as a masculine trait led to an exclusively masculine collection. But even as she constructed this masculine persona, Stein challenged and reinvented gender roles as they suited her, the mistress of her own Salon.

And yet Stein did not extend gender double standards to women as collectors. Mable Dodge and Cristobel and Ethel Cone were all American expats living in or traveling through Europe like Stein herself, and they all became interested in collecting modernist art by virtue of their relationship with Stein. The Cone sisters had been acquaintances of the Steins from Baltimore. There they had hosted a Salon that itself inspired Stein when she moved to Paris. The relationship between the two sisters looked both safe and conventional to polite society, while it also afforded them a great deal of freedom from questions about their marital status, whereabouts, and level of independence as rich women. It seems this clever masque inspired Stein and it may be that she partly modeled herself in part after Cristobel.[31]

When the Cone sisters set off for Europe to build an art collection, their first stop was Paris, at Gertrude Stein's. As friends of both Gertrude and Leo, they knew that their chances of making the right connections depended a great deal on the introductions provided at the Stein residence. Gertrude herself also knew that she could wield greater power in shaping the future of some of her friends as a collector and connoisseur if she used her relationship with the Cone sisters to launch some of these artists. In essence, these intimate relations, built in equal amount on trust and ambition, were essential in making the works of Picasso, Matisse, Juan Gris, and many other modernist artists known in the United States, where the Cone sisters brought their collection.

What does it matter that any of these people were of a particular gender, when the buying, selling, and exhibiting of innovative, modernist art became the most important long-term outcome in this story? To begin with, we need to ask ourselves: To what extent was the story of the Cone sisters unique, new, and expressive of a specific gendered aspect of how money and cultural upheaval went hand in hand at the turn of the twentieth century? The scholarship on modernism has paid relatively little attention to this issue, and it was only recently that scholars interested in women collectors and in women's various contributions in shaping the twentieth-century art scene started to connect the dots. We are familiar with the Peggy Guggenheim collections and financial generosity she lavished on her modernist artist friends.[32] Yet Guggenheim is not an exception, and before her several generations of women of wealth and ambition did indeed lay the foundations of some of the most important institutions of modern art, collections of modernist art, and thus turned modernist artists in Europe into the canonical figures they have become in the United States, from the Museum of Modern Art (MoMA) in New York City to the Chicago Art Institute. It is in the United States, rather than Europe, that this phenomenon of women philanthropists turned modernist art collectors is best known.[33]

In addition to the Cone sisters, a significant number of women collectors became active during this time in the United States. A recent study on the women collectors, philanthropists, and artists involved in the famed Armory Show presents an illuminating case study for the breadth and depth of women's specific contributions to shaping modernism.[34] Of the twenty-four donors who helped defray the costs of organizing the show, nineteen were women. Three of the five male donors gave money as a result of fundraising efforts by one particular woman, Clara Davidge.[35] Overall, the amount donated by women represents as much as 88 percent of the total funds raised to organize the exhibit.[36] That is a startling discovery, especially given the amount of hoopla around this event a few years back, when the centenary of the Armory Show was celebrated. Even after a hundred years of studying this event, such important factual evidence remains relatively unknown. I suspect it is because scholars have not bothered to look carefully before, as they either did not expect that could be the case, or they did not think it was somehow relevant. Yet this level of financial support coming from women donors is in fact unprecedented and begs for an explanation of causes, as well as implications for understanding modernism more broadly.

It seems these women donors varied greatly in their generosity and interest in modernism, and that makes the case even more interesting and revealing for larger trends. Their donations ranged from a few to thousands of dollars and came in through the efforts of especially women philanthropists and art enthusiasts who hosted events to raise interest in this exhibit.[37] In other words, what Stein was doing in Paris starting in 1903, dozens of women in New York, Boston, and Chicago were doing in the 1910s for the same cause. The extent of and motivation for getting involved varied across the heterogeneous groups of women philanthropists, but they also shared important characteristics. They tended to come from a background of some privilege, meaning they were white, urban, middle class or wealthier, and were educated.

These women also shared other more gender-specific characteristics. Many were able to act independently because they were widows and chose not to remarry or had remained unmarried.[38] In a world in which these women had been raised to become polite society ladies, for those ambitious and wanting more than a gilded cage, widowhood came as a relief sometimes. Widows had the freedom to move about without their husbands' permission and to control the inheritance they received through their husbands' will in ways they had never experienced as married women. So many did not remarry. And wealthy women like the Cone sisters decided early on that a life without a husband and children, though clearly departing from the Victorian gender roles of their day, afforded them the opportunity to use their money as their ambitions and curiosity led them, in their case to build an impressive collection of some of the most avant-garde art produced at that time.[39] In their collecting ambitions, the Cone sisters were driven by a sense of their elite position and a desire to stand on their own two feet as members of the upper class and leaders on matters of taste and new ideas. These women both implicitly and explicitly rejected the notions popular at that time that women's tastes were mediocre, veering toward the superficial and decorative, rather than the profound and artistically engaging. With consumer culture taking off at that time, and many stores catering to the middle classes through products that were increasingly standardized and "safe" in terms of their aesthetics, observers, writers, and artists (mostly men) equated this development with the sensibilities of women in general.[40] It was in part against this perception that women art collectors aimed to show their daring and vision in embracing modernist art.[41]

Some women collectors were consciously engaging in eliminating misconceptions about women's potential in the art world and obstacles against women's participation in all aspects of cultural production. They viewed such activities as part of their general involvement with women's movements for empowerment. We have the example of Mary Harriman Rumsey, the daughter of railroad magnate E. H. Harriman, who provided avenues for working-class women to safely negotiate their entry into the urban workforce.[42] There were also other philanthropists and collectors who embraced the suffragist movement and devoted their energies to women's political empowerment. Katherine Dreier, modernist artist, donor, and energetic organizer of modernist exhibits in the early decades of the twentieth century, was also a suffrage activist. She was a delegate at the Sixth Convention of the International Woman Suffrage Alliance (1911) and later led the German-American Committee of the Woman Suffrage Party in New York City.[43] As a salonière and collector, Mable Dodge was inspired by the style and diverse personalities that animated Gertrude Stein's Salon, which she had attended while in Paris. But Dodge lent her own personality and preference for specific causes, which were more socially engaged and self-consciously animated by her feminist sympathies. Her gatherings included guests like Margaret Sanger, whose activism on behalf of women's access to birth control was important for Dodge. When Sanger was arrested for her activities, Dodge turned her Salon into a safe space for the birth control activist to spread her ideas, protecting her from further punishment by the authorities.[44]

However, most of these women collectors and donors were not feminists in the twenty-first-century sense of the word, ready to make bold statements on behalf of women in general or to become patrons and philanthropists with an eye on helping especially women artists. Instead, what Cristobel Cone and many other women art collectors and philanthropists did was to turn themselves into the force of change that would eventually reshape the landscape of authority (in terms of funding) in the art world, paving the path for great acceptance of future women like Peggy Guggenheim as movers and shakers in this area of cultural activity.

The story of the strong connections between women as collectors and modernist art demonstrates that the modernist movement was a vehicle for gender empowerment. These women helped upend societal expectations regarding their abilities to command authority by means of their educated taste, financial resources, and other important organizational and management skills that went into organizing major fundraising and exhibition events. Moments like the Armory Show were opportunities for women to join in the organizational and fundraising phases of the exhibition not as secondary participants or superficial dilettantes. By 1913, women had become co-conspirators, partners, and daring pioneers who convinced other women as well as men to buy into modernist art and ideas. Knowing that a majority of the financiers (who provided up to 88 percent of the funds) and many owners[45] of works in the Armory Show were women gives us a good measure of the essential role they played in the process.

At that time, many male artists and organizers derided these women as secondary players and overly enthusiastic without evincing much expertise.[46] In truth, they spoke as men of their time, uncomfortable with the new roles these ambitious female philanthropists were arrogating themselves, as well as unaware of the extent to which the activities of individual donors reflected those of many other women, in other words, as part of an important new trend in art-collecting. Subsequently, many scholars have chosen to ignore these important issues as well.[47] But today we are able to point to the accumulation of these individual acts of generosity and daring into an important departure in gender roles facilitated precisely by the rise of modernist art and contributing significantly to the canonization of specific modernist artists.

Some of the lasting changes produced by the actions of these women collectors include the founding of the MoMA just a few years after the Armory Show by a group of women who had been involved in the organizing, fundraising, and purchasing of modernist art at that show.[48] As a flagship museum of modernism, MoMA has played an increasingly prominent role in shaping the modernist canon in the visual arts, from purchases to permanent exhibits and retrospectives. Until recently, the museum itself presented very little information about its founders. An important departure in acknowledging the role played by women in shaping the modernist canon was the publication of *Modern Women. Women Artists at the Museum of Modern Art* (2010). Its somewhat misleading title aside, the large volume presents an impressive array of studies on the women who shaped MoMA's collection, from artists to curators. Many of the studies in this volume highlight the sexism that has pervaded many decisions regarding what and how to purchase and exhibit in the museum's history, while offering examples of the ways in which feminist art and criticism have challenged these practices, especially since the 1970s.

These challenges continue, however, as evidenced by MoMA's own presentation of these issues. As of early 2015, the brief page dedicated to the history of the museum states:

In the late 1920s, three progressive and influential patrons of the arts, Miss Lillie P. Bliss, Mrs. Cornelius J. Sullivan, and Mrs. John D. Rockefeller, Jr., perceived a need to challenge the conservative policies of traditional museums and to establish an institution devoted exclusively to modern art. They, along with additional original trustees A. Conger Goodyear, Paul Sachs, Frank Crowninshield, and Josephine Boardman Crane, created The Museum of Modern Art in 1929.[49]

Though we know the actual names of Mrs. Cornelius J. Sullivan and Mrs. John D. Rockefeller, Jr. as Mary Quinn Sullivan and Abby Aldrich Rockefeller, respectively, even in 2015 MoMA did not consider it significant for the wider public to know this basic information about the individuals most important for the establishment of the museum. It remains to be seen whether the curators of the museum will take a page from the book the museum itself published and provide a gender analysis of its own history and collections.

The Whitney Museum of American Art was also the result of efforts by a team led by women—the donor and manager, respectively, of the original Whitney gallery—to cultivate interest in contemporary American art starting with the Armory Show.[50] The Museum of Art in Baltimore became a destination through the efforts and generosity of the Cone sisters, whose collection of modernist art, developed in close collaboration with the Steins in Paris, constitutes the most valuable part of the museum.[51] Similarly, the modernist collections at the Chicago Art Institute and the Boston Museum of Art began to grow through efforts made by women philanthropists who either made art donations to those institutions or, as trustees, helped guide the purchase of some of the most important pieces of those collections. Equally important for our continued research on and enhanced understanding of these historical developments are collections that were donated to teaching institutions, such as the Katherine Drier archives and art collection at Yale University.[52]

Women collectors and artists sometimes found partners among the men in their social circles. Duncan Phillips, who built his collection of modern art around the notion of developing appreciation for tradition alongside innovation, became a champion of modernist art and pioneer in promoting the vision of a number of modernist women artists.[53] Having married a talented painter, Phillips worked with his wife to develop the collection and vision for its display in Washington, D.C. In 1929 he published *A Collection in the Making*, which lays out his philosophy of appreciation and openness toward diverse visions and styles.[54] The volume includes descriptions of the 105 artists featured in the collection, among them were seven women (slightly less than 7 percent). Though by no means close to offering gender parity, which would not have been a reasonable expectation at that time, the catalogue introduced the public to Berthe Morisot, Emma Ciardi, Lillian Westcott Hale, Hermine David, Theresa Bernstein, Georgia O'Keefe, and Marjorie Phillips. If some among the American public were possibly familiar with Morisot, the rest of the group were all young and still unknown. Phillips provided rich descriptions of these women's work and suggestively invited the readers to appreciate their innovations and gendered aspects of their contributions to modernism. Of O'Keefe, in particular, he said:

A young painter of vivid personality and extraordinary skill, . . . O'Keefe "burns with a hard gem-like flame." She can be feminine and dainty, or she can be formal and austere. This makes her daring moments of flaming color and introspection all the more breath-taking.[55]

Phillips interspersed the portraits of these women artists with those of the better-known modernist male artists, displaying their works in combinations that invited comparison and facilitated appreciating the uniqueness of each artist's vision. By doing so, he helped to harmoniously usher in greater awareness of the contribution made by women to the modernist art movement. Ahead of his time and unique among other collectors, Phillips showed sensibilities toward an aesthetic of inclusion and difference that helped catapult some of these women artists into the modernist canon.

Shaping the Canon: Art Critics, Historians, Curators, and Feminist Scholars

In addition to educational opportunities and collecting, criticism and more broadly scholarship on modernism has been the most important component in shaping what the modernist canon has come to be. In the initial period of making modernism visible, critics varied from unambiguous dismissal of modernist works of art and cultural production as inartistic and obscene, to celebrations of their daring spirit. Criticism came from old and young, men and women, and praise did too. There is no simple way to summarize the variety of responses modernist exhibits, films, and literature encountered among both specialists and the wider public. The new forms of expression were often meant to be jarring and to shock as much as appeal, so the responses were similarly varied.

And yet there are clear distinctions that separate most of the early critiques and scholarship along gender lines. To illustrate the profound sexism in the early art criticism and scholarship regarding modernism, I will focus on one specific theme, the use of the nude. The female nude was an accepted theme and featured often in modernist art. Yet critics and the public received some modernist depictions of the female body with particular ire. These critiques offer us a window into the extent to which challenging established gender roles through novel depictions of the female body was something critics and the wider public recognized as valuable or out of line with the boundaries modernists were trying to push.

Two contrasting examples that elicited a great deal of press at the time will serve as an insight into this issue: Marcel Duchamp's *Nude Descending a Staircase, No. 2* (1912) and Abastenia St. Leger Eberle's *White Slave* (1913).

Both works were exhibited for the first time at the 1913 Armory Show in New York City. Duchamp's work was immediately criticized in the *New York Times* as "an explosion at a shingle factory," or as less beautiful than the Navajo rug hanging in President Theodore Roosevelt's bathroom.[56] Visitors to the Armory Show reacted negatively to the abstract, futurist depiction that had nothing to do with the expectations of the viewers to see a nude when they read the word in the title of the painting. And not any nude, a female body specifically. The voyeurism that anchored the depiction of the female body since the Renaissance had become entrenched especially in the nineteenth century, when the work of Eduard Manet and Eugene Delacroix, among others, elevated the objectification of the naked female body by the clothed male gaze to the level of artistic masterpiece.[57]

There is no indication that Duchamp had an interest in a critique of such mainstream voyeurism in the interest of altering gender norms. His focus was on the representation of movement through a static medium in a way that centered on how the mind registers movement cognitively, rather than emotionally, enjoying the muscles or other visible aspects of the sexualized naked body in motion. Duchamp critiqued the academic style of his predecessors, rather than their specific view of gender, but did so ultimately through a gendered representation of these aesthetic norms. And this is the level at which many viewers registered the novelty of his painting. They were uncomfortable with being made to think about the beauty and sensuality of the female naked body as in essence a mechanism made of muscles, bones, and skin, which could be deconstructed to show the beauty of these physical elements in motion, rather than the sensual appeal of the body as a static object.

Also on view at the Armory Show, *White Slave* was a small bronze piece by Abastenia St. Leger Eberle. Despite its minute size and lesser prominence in the show, the piece drew loud criticism as obscene in terms of the treatment of the female nude, while also eliciting applaud from some critics and attendees.[58] In 1913 Eberle was a well-established artist and better known in the United States than Duchamp. She had had a number of works exhibited in various group shows in New York City in well-regarded spaces, such as the Macbeth Gallery, where she and other female artists of the period had received a warm reception and positive reviews.[59]

Little known today, *White Slave* provided a harsh commentary on the issue of young women's sale into sexual slavery by the greedy, male-dominated trafficking networks of the day.[60] The work was produced specifically for the show after Eberle was selected to present there.[61] Eberle gambled on her selection and reputation to make a strong feminist statement against child prostitution through one of the pieces she exhibited, a rare political position at the Armory Show. Radical innovation in technique and aesthetics, as represented by Duchamp's painting, became the most discussed issue in the

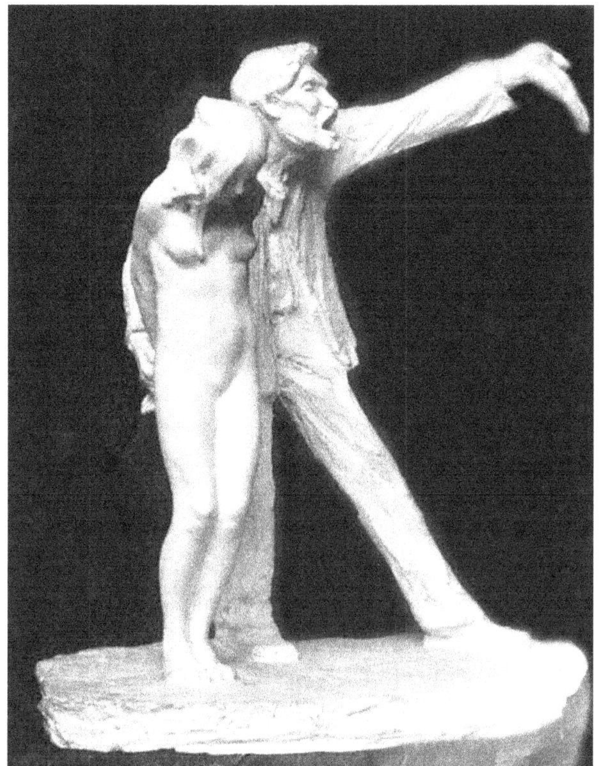

FIGURE 6 *Abastenia St. Leger Eberle,* White Slave. *1913. Photo published as cover page,* The Survey *(May 3, 1913).*

long term. Yet Eberle was just as bold in her choice of bringing feminist politics into the show. As a lifelong activist on behalf of social justice, Eberle had spent a great deal of time studying, living with, and depicting the poor, the immigrants of New York City, and especially the young women and children who suffered the greatest abuses, inclusive of human trafficking. She acknowledged being influenced by Jane Addams, and she marched for women's political equality.[62] Eberle's political intentions are best illuminated by her own words:

> The artist has no right to work as an individualist without responsibility to others. . . . More than almost any other sort of work is art dependent on society of inspiration, material, life itself, and in that same measure does it owe society a debt. The artist must see for people—reveal them to themselves and to each other.[63]

What Eberle wished to reveal through her sculpture was an ugly contemporary truth. Her aspirations were connected to shaking up viewers' moral conscience, rather than engaging in any theoretical experiments with perspective and abstraction, as was the case with Duchamp.

White Slave was not particularly innovative at that time in terms of specific style or technique, especially by comparison with the work of Brâncuşi or Duchamp. By the same token, there were many other male sculptors in the exhibition whose depiction of female nudes was stylistically in the same family as Eberle's, most of them tributaries to Auguste Rodin's school of sculpture. In short, the work was considered important as an example of modernist sculpture less because of her innovation in style, and more because of the theme and very blunt approach to it. Eberle was not afraid to point a finger at the contemporary gender double standard and the unchecked abuse of women by men as objects of sexual desire. The contrast between the pubescent nude female body and the grotesque clothed male body was what shook up critics and the wider public, as it exposed the reality of power differences in gender relations. Eberle also chose to publish an image of the sculpture on the cover of a progressive journal a couple of months after the closing of the exhibit in New York, in connection to a short story on the subject of white slavery. The cover of the journal also elicited strong responses, suggesting that Eberle touched a nerve with many Americans.[64] Eberle was unable to sell the work and *White Slavery* was subsequently destroyed, which suggests that, overall, the American public was not ready to appreciate this sort of sociocultural feminist challenge.

Eberle's star as a modernist artist faded just as Duchamp's rose. Even though both attracted a great deal of attention in 1913, by 1963, when the first large monograph dedicated to the Armory Show's legacies for twentieth-century art appeared as part of the shows' jubilee anniversary, Eberle had disappeared from the story, while Duchamp had become a central figure for describing the long-term impact of the exhibit. In fact, in his *Story of the Armory Show* Milton Brown chose to completely ignore any gendered elements of this pioneering exhibit, inclusive of the sizable number of women who exhibited there and the subsequent rise to prominence of a number of women artists, from Marie Laurencin to Marguerite Zorach.

Art historians like Brown have done as much for the canonization (and invisibility, respectively) of some modernist figures and innovations as collectors and art critics who observed these movements in their own times. It is not my intention here to rehearse the development of the art history discipline as an area of scholarship with deep structural sexist elements. But starting in the 1970s, feminist scholars, artists, and activists have offered sometimes incisive and sometimes purely polemical arguments against these entrenched practices, and scholars interested in modernism have chosen, in various degrees, to respond to these criticisms.[65] In the wake of the rise of the new-left in academia at that time and of the women's liberation movements more broadly, the invisibility of these women artists and of gendered aspects of modernism have been critiqued time and again.

The shift in art history scholarship toward greater interest in sociopolitical and even economic aspects of art education, production, as well as reception has also opened up new avenues for interrogating gender norms and expectations, both on the part of the phenomena and people who are the subject of research and on the part of the scholars engaging in these analyses.[66] More recently, the poststructural turn moved the analyses of modernism toward questions about identity and discourse. This scholarship has shifted the research agenda toward analyses of discursive practices as embodiments of power relations.[67]

Today, the sheer amount of scholarship dedicated to modernism has grown so expansive that its contributions cannot be summarized in any simple way, because there is no consensus over anything beyond a basic timeline and a few hundred towering figures included in the canon. Still, when it comes to modernism and gender specifically, in most studies dedicated to modernism the words "gender" or "women" are rarely, if ever, terms considered significant enough to be indexed.[68] Some synthetic works include a chapter on gender, but a thorough integration of gender analysis is still rare among such studies.

It is equally baffling to see that new museums and exhibits dedicated to modernist artists or groupings offer no critique of the representations of gender norms or of the marginalization of women artists. The Magritte Museum invoked at the beginning of the book is a good example of this sort of selective amnesia. Magritte's obsession with female sexuality is in evidence in every room of this large museum. His depictions of his wife's naked body are a leitmotif throughout his career, and yet somehow, the curators did not see any reason to discuss this theme as an integral component of the museum's permanent exhibit. Instead, we have a loosely biographical and chronological breakdown of this work. Any concern with gender is absent from the narrative of the exhibit, even regarding anxieties about his own masculinity as expressed in his painting. I contend that such choices to resist uncomfortable critiques of these celebrated modernist figures are directly connected to the commodification of modernism, especially with the advent of mass globalized tourism. Simply put, it is easier to render reproductions of Magritte's work and other objects based on his art appealing for mass consumption if one insists less on the sexism of this work than if one draws attention to it, especially when a large part of the people who visit the museum and make purchases at the museum shop are women.

Some feminist works dedicated to critiquing the modernist canon tend to want to make women and women's concerns visible, without explicitly interrogating the structural and discursive frameworks that underpin the continued masculinist exclusivist attributes of the canon.[69] This "adding women and stirring" is somewhat helpful in making us more familiar with the work of these women, but it does little to address the larger issue of how "radical change" has been defined in relationship to modernism.

More recently, feminist historians have started to turn the focus on making women visible into deeper critiques of how visibility and invisibility are constructed.[70] By doing so, these studies provoke us to think differently about what exactly counts as innovative versus traditional, where radical changes can be recognized and where change is intermingled with resistance to change, especially when it comes to assumptions about gender norms, creativity, and sensibility.

Joining these critiques, my book moves the study of modernism and gender in yet a new direction. Up to now my analysis has focused on the extent to which modernism and self-described modernists showed interest in or demonstrated an inclination toward critiquing gender norms as an integral component of their revolt against traditions and the established institutions of the day. Yet my interest lies also in interrogating the relationship between modernism and gender from the perspective of gender innovations that have not yet been associated with modernism. In the last part of this study, I turn the tables on the question of whether modernists were interested in gender revolt and ask: What movements and individuals interested in gender revolts, who have thus far not been integrated in the core analyses of modernism, should in fact be an integral part of that story, rather than footnotes or sidebars?

4

A New Set of Criteria: Rebellion, Rejection, and Reimagining Gender

It may be useful at this point to revisit the definition of modernism I offered at the beginning of this book, as inspired by Griffin's expanded field of inquiry. According to this definition, modernism is a way of thinking that "encourages the artist/intellectual to collaborate proactively with collective movements for radical change and projects for the transformation of social realities and political systems."[1] During the period of analysis encompassed by this book, many different movements for radical change developed throughout the world, and some of them aimed explicitly at altering gender norms. Many more focused on other issues, but implicitly considered gender roles and suggested important changes. Without being exhaustive, as there are truly too many such movements to consider them all here, I provide examples from the most important sociopolitical movements that focused on gender as a core component of their rally to bring about radical change. Included in this category are: the suffrage movements (one type of feminism I will focus on), psychology, sexology, nudism, and eugenics. I will also provide several revealing examples from the much larger second category of implicit engagement with gender norms. I will focus on the anarchist and communist movements, and provide some comments on fascism, though much of what I offer about fascism as modernist in terms of gender norms is encompassed in the discussion about eugenics.

The Suffragists

Feminism of the suffragist flavor predated modernism, so the first question is whether there are new developments in the aims, ideas, and means that define the suffrage movements starting in the late nineteenth century that align suffragist activism with modernism. As scholars have shown effectively, this period encompasses important shifts in the radicalness of the suffrage movement, so I will provide a number of examples to demonstrate these changes.[2] Not all suffragists were radical in their demands, however, nor did they always engage in radical forms of propaganda and political theater. In my discussion I focus only on examples of radicalism that combined political aspirations to change gender norms with modernist aesthetics, from style to method of communication.

Recent scholarship on the suffrage movement draws connections between the suffrage movement as it evolved in the first decades of the twentieth century and the performative rebelliousness of modernist writers and artists in reaction to the established tropes and institutions of the late nineteenth century. In *Making Noise, Making News: Suffrage Print Culture and U.S. Modernism*, Mary Chapman argues that suffragist street performances built on and contributed to modernism, from marching to selling (read "shouting") suffragist pamphlets, together with new forms of print propaganda, blending pamphlet with crisp and direct journalistic writing. Suffragists had marched on behalf of their ideas for a long time, but by the turn of the century, these marches gained new performative elements. The suffragists looked more heterogeneous than their very respectable predecessors, who had adopted a strategy of showing how unthreatening women were to men in their demands to gain the vote. Victorian-era suffragists had dressed in white and wore large hats and parasols as befitting their class (and in places like the United States, their race).[3] By the 1900s they were joined by immigrants and more racially diverse activists, working-class women, and other participants from a variety of social backgrounds. They comprised a heterogeneous, colorful, and overall more raucous set of networks than their predecessors. Some suffragists still believed that only behavior considered appropriate for their gender would open the doors of the male establishment. Yet others had grown weary of the sexist critiques leveled against suffragists at that time, that women were not rational enough to become fully empowered citizens. The noisy marches that became more common after the turn of the century were a direct reaction against the lack of engagement by the male establishment with the issues raised by the suffragists. If propriety did not get their attention, then noise, irony, and ventriloquism might. The suffrage marches combined loud attention-calling shouts with pantomime-like tableaux that were meant to draw attention to historical or contemporary women's issues through such contrasts.[4] Messaging through banners, blackboards, pamphlets, or stenciled bags accompanied the loud noises made by these suffragists.

The marches that grew in size and variety of expression throughout the 1910s borrowed freely from other contemporary movements, from the labor union activists of the day to anarchists and other radical groupings. Among the more radical actions undertaken by these new generations of suffragists was vandalizing art works that objectified women. In 1913, Mary Richardson walked into the National Gallery in Trafalgar Square, London, with a large knife and cut up *Rokeby Venus*, a very valuable painting by the seventeenth-century Spanish artist Velasquez. She then released the following message:

> I have tried to destroy the picture of the most beautiful woman in mythological history as a protest against the Government for destroying Mrs. Pankhurst, who is the most beautiful character in modern history. Justice is an element of beauty as much as colour and outline on canvas. Mrs. Pankhurst seeks to procure justice for womanhood, and for this she is being slowly murdered by a Government of Iscariot politicians. If there is an outcry against my deed, let every one remember that such an outcry is an hypocrisy so long as they allow the destruction of Mrs. Pankhurst and other beautiful living women, and that until the public cease to countenance human destruction, the stones cast against me for the destruction of this picture are each an evidence against them of artistic as well as moral and political humbug and hypocrisy.[5]

Richardson aimed to force her contemporaries to contemplate their own hypocrisy in identifying beauty solely with women's bodies, rather than their whole moral self. She cast these attitudes as squarely out of step with the legitimate aspirations of modern women. Her violent action was an extension of this moral point. By destroying the product of male fantasies about women, she was forcing them to face the reality of contemporary, fully embodied women.

Her critique could be seen as calling out contemporary artists as well: by cutting up this painting, Richardson was holding the art world complicit in the unjust objectification of women, and hence morally bankrupt as expression of modern sensibilities. To Richardson, these paintings could not be considered beautiful because of their profound double standard—the narrowness of the appreciation of the gender most held up as the symbol of beauty. Her definition of beauty in contemporary society correlated with the respect for women in all matters of public discourse, while her definition of ugliness was aligned with the oppression of women at the hands of the contemporary "Iscariot politicians."

During that period, many leading women artists and intellectuals engaging in aesthetic experimentation actively participated in the suffrage movement.

They were not necessarily leaders of the groups in which they participated, but they were able to express themselves in line with their artistic sensibilities and thus they found a welcoming environment where modernism became synonymous with women's more active presence in the arts and with a voice that enjoined suffragists in challenging the existing gender norms as outdated and fundamentally out of line with the modern world.

A revealing example of the connections feminists were making between their political and artistic commitments is the work of Louise Weiss, one of the most prominent women activists and political figures in twentieth-century France. Weiss arrived at her suffragist activism relatively late in life, having been a feminist journalist of pacifist convictions after the end of the First World War. Weiss had participated in the war as a medical volunteer, and after 1918 delved into building up a culture of trust between France and Germany through the transnational weekly she founded and edited for over a decade, *La Nouvelle Europe*.[6] The journal featured feminist articles by Weiss and others during its first year, but subsequently focused more on diplomatic and international financial issues.

Disillusioned with the results of her efforts on behalf of reconciliation and peace, by the mid-1930s Weiss turned her attention fully toward the cause of women's suffrage. She founded the organization the New Woman and wrote a provocative feminist novel, *Deliverance* (1936), which narrated some of Weiss' own frustrations as a professional woman faced with the gender norms of the day and the negative effects of the First World War and its aftermath for women of her generation.[7] Having attempted to enhance women's lives after the war by advocating for better educational opportunities in the professions, as well as retaining the female working force employed after men returned from the front, Weiss came to the conclusion that women would never be able to gain these new opportunities without full political rights.

Like other radical suffragists of this period, she used political theater to get her message across. She ran for a seat in Parliament, despite her inability to either serve or vote. Though her message was broadcast broadly and the left-wing Popular Front was in power, the proposal to enfranchise women was defeated for a third time in 1936. Weiss was finally able to live her dream of being an elected politician when she became a member of the European Parliament in 1979.[8]

As the Great War came to show, the New Woman became common presence from Moscow to Manhattan. If before 1914 the gendered norms of propriety among the "respectable" classes still claimed that upright women did not belong on the street, the massive entry of women into employment and other forms of public assistance that the state badly needed during the war changed the gender playing field. The backlash that ensued after 1918, when traumatized male veterans returned from the front in droves, was swift and has been well documented by many scholars.[9] Yet, once Pandora's box had been opened, it could not be shut down completely. Suffrage activists had gained a different level of confidence based on the experiences women had during the war, of both greater economic independence and greater vulnerability at the hands of the various wartime regimes. Many suffragists came to the conclusion that it was foolish to depend on the state to address disparities; women needed to build their own networks to sustain their struggle. The communities of interest they forged and continued through the war helped suffrage activists to continue to advocate for women's political rights after 1918.

Some suffrage proponents joined other radical movements, from the Communist parties that were on the rise in Germany, Hungary, and especially Russia, to anarchist and pacifist groupings.[10] Other suffragists hitched their cause to right-wing movements, some more "respectably" liberal, others of an ethnocentric and anti-Semitic flavor, such as some of the eugenics movements in Poland, Romania, or Hungary.[11] Yet most suffragists remained dedicated to their cause and the networks of women they had helped develop independently. While the vote was finally extended to all women in 1920 in the United States, French women did not gain the vote until 1945, despite a number of women-friendly regimes during the interwar period.

In Eastern Europe, the feminist suffrage movement was particularly radical in its modernist assertions.[12] These societies still favored very traditional gender roles well into the twentieth century, and those women who, like Ceclia Cuţescu-Stork, enjoyed the privilege of traveling abroad for education, became vectors for interrogating gender roles once these women returned home. Irena Krzywicka wrote feminist novels and promoted women's access to birth control through a free clinic she opened in Warsaw.[13] Vilma Glücklich dedicated her life to developing better resources and access to education for Hungarian girls and promoting women's full political rights as head of the Hungarian Feminist Association and editor of the *Feminist Bulletin* (1906).[14] Thousands of such courageous and dedicated feminists worked to empower women in their societies and became significant pioneers for modernization and change in gender norms.

It is my contention that as a movement that generated mass appeal for individuals with such diverse backgrounds and experiences, the feminist suffrage movement of the early twentieth century was also a modernist movement: it critiqued traditions, socioeconomic institutions, and the sexist culture dominant at that time, and proposed to transform the sociopolitical realities by demanding that women be given the same rights as men. Doubling the size of the electorate overnight, adding the diverse population encompassed by all the women in a particular country, and eliminating a host of legal restrictions that were at the core of the values and traditions of middle-class respectability in the nineteenth century was nothing short of working "proactively with collective movements for radical change of social realities and political systems," Griffin's expanded definition of modernism.

Psychology

The discipline of psychology grew out of the same intellectual disquiet toward the end of the nineteenth century that helped bring about other modernist innovations.[15] Though focusing on the mind rather than the body, psychologists connected physical and specifically sexual and gender norms to the development of the mind. I have already mentioned Freud's work, but many other psychologists of this early period of the discipline focused their attention on how gender norms conditioned behavior and interrogated the extent to which gender norms were a result of psychological "hard wiring." In essence, the birth of psychology represents the birth of the nature versus nurture debate about gender roles in relation to specific values assigned to terms such as "feminine" and "masculine." Eugenics also contributed to this debate around the same time, via the question of inherited traits. But psychology was the first discipline to directly connect the shaping of gender roles with learned behavior transmitted from parents to children.

The discipline of psychology started as an open field of inquiry without any hegemonic theories to dominate it. Today, many still identify Freud and Carl Jung as the two towering theorists who helped determine the framework of analysis and assumptions about the relationship between behavior and biology through the mind.[16] Yet during the early twentieth century, other important trends coexisted with Freud's theories and contested his ideas. Unsurprisingly, one of his most important critics was a feminist psychologist, Karen Horney, who spent her life advocating for understanding neuroses and a variety of other psychological dysfunctions as learned behavior, a function of sociocultural norms and relations, rather than of biologically founded sexual attributes. To Freud's theory about penis envy as an explanation for women's specific gender identity, Horney counterposed the notion that men could have "womb envy," pointing toward women's abilities to be caretakers and men's inadequacies in this realm.[17]

Horney was able to pursue her ambition of being educated and becoming a doctor because she happened to be among the first generation of women admitted to medical school and was able to take the medical examinations afterward, with German medical schools lifting interdictions for women to sit in for these exams around 1900.[18] Before psychology became a well-established specialization in medical schools and the professional establishment, women had a window of opportunity to help shape the field in a less masculinist fashion than the research done in other areas. Horney dared to do so, and she had some success in her efforts, though it is clear today that her views did not prevail in the long term vis-à-vis Freud's. The differences she espoused vis-à-vis the growingly prominent Freud rendered Horney a less popular leading figure in the discipline, especially her uncompromising feminism when it came to rejecting Freud's sexist assumptions about what was "normal" (read masculine) versus "derivative" (read feminine).

She left Germany for the United States in the mid-1920s, and then moved around to Chicago and eventually New York. She founded the Association for the Advancement of Psychoanalysis to create a professional network for the kind of approach and theories she advocated for, in contrast to Freud's followers, and eventually established the *American Journal of Psychoanalysis*. As Freud's following grew (they were predominantly men), the Freudian theories about gender norms and sexuality gained prominence at the expense of Horney's critiques. Her arguments and ideas were slowly marginalized in subsequent courses and textbooks. Feminist psychology saw a revival only in the 1960s.[19]

Sexology

While psychologists often aimed to understand the life of the mind by connecting behavior to specific gender or sexual attributes, other scientists with an interest in the same questions founded the discipline of sexology. The discipline evolved out of research done by biologists, especially eugenicists, as well as psychologists. Kraft-Ebing, whose contributions have already been mentioned, was a prominent early figure in this field, with an outlook on questions of norms and deviance that supported Victorian values. Around the same time as he was publishing *Sexual Psychopathy: A Clinical-Forensic Study* (1886), his much-discussed book on sexual pathologies, other scientists were offering analyses and definitions of normal and abnormal sexuality that provided important departures from the sexual norms of the nineteenth century.[20] From the many individuals who helped shape the modernist discourses on sexuality, I will analyze the work of Magnus Hirschfeld and Marie Stopes.

Hirschfeld is considered the father of the modern gay movement.[21] Trained as a doctor, he began his career as a general practitioner but soon shifted his focus to presenting homosexuality as a type of normal identity within a broad spectrum of sexual behavior, focusing on the naturalness of gay eroticism. Hirschfeld's most important contribution in terms of aiming to revolutionize existing sociocultural gender norms was his insistence that homosexuality was an identity, rather than pathology, and that homosexual eroticism was part of the normal spectrum of sexual desires people experience throughout their lives. Hirschfeld worked his entire life to eliminate the cultural prejudices against homosexuals, as well as to decriminalize sodomy, which had become illegal in 1871 in Germany. The petition he initiated to request the decriminalization of sodomy was signed by over 5,000 people; among them were some of the most prominent modernist luminaries of the day: Käthe Kollwitz, Thomas Mann, Herman Hesse, and Stefan Zweig, as well as other prominent sexologists such as Krafft-Ebing.

Hirschfeld generated a number of important institutions that helped normalize and further open up the field of gay studies and advocacy into the interwar period. In 1897 he founded the Scientific-Humanitarian Committee, which became the most important vehicle for research on and advocacy for the gay community. At its height the Committee had twenty-five branches and over 500 members in Germany, Austria, and the Netherlands. Between 1899 and 1923, the group published the *Yearbook for Intermediate Sexual Types*, whose aim was to produce high-quality research on nonheterosexual behavior, long before Alfred Kinsey's famous studies.[22]

Hirschfeld also reached out to radical feminists to join forces in addressing specific issues pertaining to the lesbian community. Unlike most other pioneers in this field, he saw important commonalities between his own advocacy on behalf of homosexuality and the work of radical feminists who were pushing for women's suffrage and for ending discrimination against women in economic and educational practices.[23] Though lesbians were not subjected to the same criminalization of their sexual lives as gay men, they confronted many forms of discrimination as women. When a proposal came before the German Parliament in 1909, Hirschfeld worked closely with Helene Stöcker to successfully prevent the law criminalizing gay sex from extending to lesbian sex. Moreover, he joined the League for the Protection of Mothers, which Stöcker founded in 1905, and actively supported the organization's quest for decriminalizing abortion and eliminating obstacles against mothers' and married women's full access to employment in education and civil service.[24]

Hirschfeld's work is of great importance as a pioneering effort that encouraged the gay community to become more visible and active in politics and to thoroughly challenge heteronormativity in gender roles. Yet his publications, speeches, and other activities were less known during his day than the publications of Marie Stopes, who became one of the first best-sellers among sex advice writers, and the first woman to gain such a broad readership. Though reviled by many historians today, she remains an important pioneer within the field of sexology, with a long-lasting impact for how we understand women's sexuality today. An extraordinarily gifted student, Stopes was trained in biology and geology and graduated with a bachelor degree in two years. At the age of twenty-five she received a doctor of science degree. In 1904 she became the first woman to serve as a faculty member at the University of Manchester, in the Department of Paleobotany.

Her academic research interests had nothing to do with sexology, but her personal experience of an unhappy and sexually frustrating married life led Stopes to thoroughly research the marriage code and to begin writing *Married Love or Love in Marriage* (1918). During the years of researching and writing this book, Stopes came to be a vociferous and unrelenting advocate for women's full agency in marriage as partners in every aspect of the relationship. Having grown up in such a household, she had taken this attitude for granted, but her own relationships with men led her to understand the larger structural inequalities that undergirded gender relations, and in particular erotic intimacy.

Married Love is a book that appears both conservative and revolutionary, depending on the perspective of the reader. In many ways, Stopes was a woman of her time. She opposed abortion and articulated her views of birth control through the fashionable "race hygiene," that is, eugenicist discourse of the day.[25] She was also an advocate of marriage and respectability, rather than free love. And she was very clear about the book being aimed at "normal" couples, meaning heterosexual married ones. But she also wrote in unprecedented ways about the importance of treating marriage as a partnership between two autonomous individuals, arguing for women's full agency in matters of their sexuality. In the introduction to the book, she clarified what profound misperceptions of female sexuality she was writing against: "the amazing statement of a distinguished American gynecologist, who said, 'I do not believe mutual pleasure in the sexual act has any particular bearing on the happiness of life.'"[26] This doctor did not deny that men's sexual desires were normal; it was the question of the *mutual*, read women's pleasure, that he found irrelevant for the couple's happiness (or women's in particular), and that is what Stopes rallied against.

As with other contributions by women to the modernist movement, one needs to understand *Married Love* in terms of the distance the author was traveling with that book from established gender norms and especially women's sexuality toward new ideas and practices. That the book was not published for years after it was completed because it was deemed obscene or risqué, tells us a great deal about what was considered acceptable at that time for a woman author in particular; because the scandal about Stopes' book revolved not only around what it said, but also who said it.

Married Love became an instant mega-success, selling out five editions just in 1918, when it was finally published. By 1931, the book had sold over 750,000 copies, and it could not even be purchased in the United States until after that date, when the charge of obscenity initially leveled against it was finally lifted.[27]

Within four years, a survey of American academics listed *Married Love* among the twenty-five most influential books published in the previous fifty years, ahead of Freud's *Interpretation of Dreams*, among other notable titles.[28]

The most important contributions of the book in terms of upending gender norms had to do with the clear language and unapologetic style of the text, meant to become a manual for both men and women, rather than a scientific treatise. If men's sexuality and erotic desires had been the subject of many ruminations—scientific or artistic—for a long time, presenting women as subjects of erotic desires and their needs as sexual partners as deserving the attention of public discussion and intimate action was completely new. The distance from taboo to open discussion made this book a revolutionary one in terms of legitimating women's subjecthood and agency as fully sexual beings. The book offered a vocabulary for the desires, fears, and frustrations women had not felt they could articulate before. And its delayed publication might have been a blessing in disguise, for by 1918 many more women were in fact looking for such a vocabulary, having become more economically self-sufficient and overall culturally daring over the years of the war.

Both *Married Life* and Stopes' subsequent work advocated for women's access to birth control, though not abortion, which she never approved of. In particular, she opened over five birth control clinics, partly inspired by Margaret Sanger's activities in the same area.[29] She also researched and helped popularize a number of birth control techniques (primarily *coitus interruptus*) and products, such as the sponge. Her clinics were open to any married women, regardless of class, ethnicity, or race, and offered its services free of charge. The subsequent legalization of birth control and the enhancement of millions of women's lives in the United Kingdom and many other places in Europe can be traced back to these pioneering efforts.

Stopes was a complex figure, however, and her rebelliousness was not without morally problematic aspects. She expressed anti-Semitic and xenophobic views in relation to Germany and Russia, even though she also traveled to Nazi Germany in 1935 for an international eugenics congress. Her support of eugenics also extended to advocating for sterilization of the weak and feebleminded, which betrayed both racism and elitism in relation to working-class women. In all those ways, Stopes was very much of her time.

Eugenics

The case for eugenics as modernist has been made elsewhere,[30] and this section only focuses on one specific aspect of the theories and activities of eugenics supporters: their view regarding gender norms in relation to the radical changes they advocated for society moving forward. Stopes is a good example of how some eugenicists did in fact advocate for reimagining gender roles and specifically women's role in the family, reproduction, and in society at large, with race and class as important elements of defining gender. The question is, to what extent do Stopes' ideas about female sexuality represent a prominent segment of the eugenics movement?

The existing research on this topic is not extensive, as relatively few historians of eugenics have been interested in looking at the specific notions about gender identity and roles advocated by this movement.[31] But we know that women supporters of eugenics were much more interested than men in reimagining the role women were playing in society in relation to the threats and opportunities described by eugenicist theories. The extent of the radicalness of such ideas and the support they received is also relative to the place where the supporters lived. In the United Kingdom, middle-class women like Stopes advocated on behalf of birth control as a means to reduce overpopulation by especially lower classes. There, women had been pushing for a more visible and autonomous role in society and the family for a long time. In other places, like Romania, it was also women of the respectable elite who became interested in eugenics.[32] But their interest in this movement was spurred not only by race/ ethnically inflected gender norms, but also by the lack of other opportunities for women to become active in broad social projects, something elite women in Great Britain from Stopes' generation could not complain about. The distance for Romanian women between the invisibility they faced in the public arena, on the one hand, and their aims to become partners, heard and seen, in the eugenics movement , on the other hand, was far greater than for women who joined the eugenics bandwagon in England. And these Romanian elite women were of their times, even more than their counterparts in Britain.

The most important connection between eugenics overall and gender norms is the foundational assumption on the part of eugenicists that reproduction is a biopolitical act.[33] By placing sexuality at the center of political preoccupations, eugenicists insisted on the need to define individuals and their relations to each other as well as to the state through their erotic behavior, something unprecedented in the ideological discursive field of the nineteenth century. Until the rise of eugenics in the 1880s, certain types of sexual acts deemed "abnormal" or "immoral" had been regulated or criminalized. But the laws and discussions around them skirted around the issue of what "normal" was, defined usually by the absence of interference on the part of the state with those populations. Starting in the late nineteenth century, eugenics redefined the sexual "normal" as well as its "deviations" comprehensively, for all men and women, with expansive dimensions of political and moral responsibility toward other people and the state across generations. The state was to assume an important regulatory role, not just through legislation, but also through other disciplining institutions, from hospitals to asylums and prisons. This was, in fact, the most revolutionary act of rebelliousness of the eugenicists: transforming the state into the total executioner of prevailing views of the rising scientific elite, with all the racist and elitist baggage the members of that elite carried.

The definitions employed by eugenicist advocates were increasingly limiting and narrow in their understanding of the "normal." Basically, for both men and women only heterosexual activities inside marriage with the purpose of reproducing were regarded as appropriate and responsible. All other individual expressions of sexuality, from masturbation to sex with multiple partners, and from taking on an appearance that in anyway disturbed heteronormative expectations, were generally deemed as irresponsible and dysgenic.[34] And of course, all the rules about individual sexual actions were circumscribed to those who were ethnically or racially deemed "healthy," which might exclude, depending on the place and time, all ethnic minorities, racial minorities, religious minorities, or lower classes.

The politicized definition of men's normal sexual behavior and responsibility offered by eugenicists was certainly unprecedented.[35] And if we understand the definition of modernism to encompass attempts at mobilizing people collectively with the goal of radically altering social relations and politics, eugenicist definitions of normal masculinity certainly fit that description. According to most proponents of eugenics, men's sexuality was naturally aggressive and expansive, but needed to be "channeled" through social incentives and, in some cases, legal disincentives toward the goal of reproducing the healthy "biological capital." Masturbation and homosexual activities were considered dysgenic.

Some eugenicists went so far as to describe what a "proper" masculine man was to look like, walk like, and act like: "normal" virility would be visible through the presence of facial and bodily hair, through broad shoulders and a resolute walk, and through clothing that would not be too tight fitting. In short, any inkling of effeminacy, from hair that was combed, cut, or colored in a particular way, to clothing and body posture, was identified as "abnormal" and thus to be frowned upon or even questioned publicly.[36] The eugenicists who wrote about masculinity in this way sometimes pushed for legislation to enforce such strictures. More often than not, these writings were meant to generate public awareness and pressure against homosexual activities and persons. In essence, this view made more explicit and narrowed down Victorian norms of masculinity, while tying them more closely to individual political rights and duties in the modern state, as well as to the legitimacy of state power to regulate individual behavior.

On the matter of extramarital sex, eugenicists expressed various views in terms of how men would be held accountable for purported dysgenic behavior.

In some places, the double standard of turning a blind eye to prostitution continued into the interwar period.[37] Those eugenicists simply stated that men were "naturally" more sexually aggressive than women, and that they turned to sex workers to satisfy such urges. Eugenicists ended up working on the regulation of sex work to some extent to the benefit of sex workers, who were deemed either "necessary evils" or "fallen women" who needed social support rather than jail terms. Yet other eugenicists began to insist that extramarital sex was dangerous for the biological "capital" and both publicly shamed men who engaged in it and fined them for engaging in sex with prostitutes.[38]

In terms of women's roles in the family, society, and the modern state, eugenicists displayed a broad range of views. For many male doctors and other proponents of this theory, women represented a fundamental intergenerational link that needed to be thoroughly controlled in order to insure the greatest likelihood of securing the health of the nation, in part because they held the twin conviction that women were less rational than men by virtue of their biology. Most eugenicist public programs and legislation focused on women's bodies, rather than men's—from premarital and prenatal counseling to sterilization. So what, if anything, was new in the ways eugenicists imagined femininity, by comparison to their Victorian predecessors? Not much, it turns out, for most male leading figures of eugenics.

However, some of the women who became ardent supporters of eugenics joined this movement with new aspirations for themselves and women in general, and translated them into different programs than those advocated by the male leadership. We have already seen how Marie Stopes used eugenicist ideas to advocate for women's sexual agency in marriage as partners rather than objects of desire. Other women in places as far away from each other as Romania and India also found ways to turn eugenics into a movement that could become empowering for women.[39] For many of these activists, the majority of whom were middle-upper class, well-educated women, eugenics offered scientific and thus incontrovertible evidence that women needed to be considered as full partners in building the health of the nation and thus they needed to be granted greater authority and respect in public life. Some advocated for women's suffrage;[40] others used eugenicist arguments to advocate for women's access to and control over birth control;[41] yet others advocated for new types of educational and professional opportunities for women as a means to discipline the future.[42]

For these ambitious women, the advantage presented by eugenics was that it did not have the same tinge of rebelliousness as outright feminism. For societies where feminism was regarded with great distrust, eugenics seemed to provide a convenient venue for promoting some of the same reforms for women. Some of these women activists also embraced eugenics with its most racist and xenophobic implications. Ultimately, eugenics provided at least a self-limiting avenue for some advocates of women's rights to push for more empowering roles for women in society. At worse, the eugenics movement rearticulated gender inequality and heteronormativity in more oppressive ways and with tragic effects for women as well as many men. In countries where sterilization laws were passed (including the United States), women have been disproportionately the objects of such restrictive policies, counting for as much as 75 percent of the total number of people who were sterilized.[43] Though modernist in terms of its radical consequences for women's bodies, eugenics was a fundamentally antidemocratic movement when it came to redefining gender roles and practices.

Nudism

Like eugenics, nudism developed as a theory and practice that sometimes emphasized a return to tradition, and at other times focused on the ways in which the naked body embodied specific values linked to modernity. Promoters of nudism positioned themselves in various ways on the political spectrum, from anti-Semitic diatribes celebrating the beauty of the "Nordic type" to a universal humanism that embraced every type of naked body.[44] Regardless of these important differences, the growth of an organized movement that introduced the practice of nudism around the turn of the twentieth century and especially after the First World War represents an important and rather under-researched aspect of modernism, especially in matters of reimagining gender roles. My attention will focus on two contrasting strains of this movement: the feminist *Nacktkultur,* as advocated by Bess Mensendieck, and the better-known *Nacktkultur* advocated by people like Hans Süren, whose allegiances were radically right-wing.

Süren was one of the most popular promoters of *Nacktkultur* in the Weimar period, and, as a member of the Nazi Party, he remained equally popular after 1933. His best-seller was *Man and Sun* (1924), which sold over a quarter of a million copies. Süren advocated nudism as a form of developing a healthy lifestyle, and particularly in reaction to the lack of exposure to sun and air in the modern, industrialized society. His books articulated the need to shed many trappings of modern society in order to preserve one's health and strength in the modern world. Yet Süren's depiction of the nude body and the activities he advocated to become healthier did not imply a return to any traditions or to a natural state. Nudist practices would promote engagement with modernity through a healthy lifestyle, a practice limited to those who were considered eugenically "good stock."[45]

Süren encouraged strenuous noncompetitive physical activities from hiking to weight lifting as a means to cultivate a healthy body. In his best-seller book, images of women's bodies were segregated from men's, which one scholar considers evidence that Süren wished to avoid any eroticizing elements.[46] The intent to avoid hetero-eroticism might have been there. However, given the ample evidence that both homoeroticism and voyeurism were widespread at that time in Germany, the huge commercial success of the book cannot be attributed solely to the readers' interest in contemplating healthy lifestyles and hiking in the nude. The impact of the book needs to be considered both in relation to the author's intentions and in relation to the reception of the book by a large and diverse readership.

Süren advocated for segregated activities by gender and for specific types of activity for each group—dance for women and more strenuous bodybuilding for men. In short, he described these bodies as both radically different from each other and in need of being disciplined through the specificities that the muscle structure and other elements of their hereditary-gendered physiology dictated. The ethno-racial elements of these naked bodies are clearly present in all of the illustrations of the book, and leave no doubt that for Süren beauty was not just gendered, but it was racially defined to include only the same Aryan types that became the standards advocated by the Nazi regime. Some scholars have underscored the classless, nonelitist elements of Süren's depictions of the nude body and implicitly of a healthy modern lifestyle, because of the nondescript outside setting of his photos.[47] That may be the case, but there is no doubt that race trumped class for Süren, and in that regard his implicit framing of health, modernity, and gender roles are much more in line with the reactionary modernism of the Nazis than with any other attempts to reimagine the modern body.[48]

Supporters of nudism included not only reactionary modernists, but also radical feminists, among them Bess Mensendieck, an American who spent most of her adult life in Europe. Mensendieck became one of the earliest advocates of a system of body exercises focused specifically on women, combining concerns for health, strength, functionality, and overall women's ability to understand and fully appreciate themselves as autonomous and fully functioning modern beings.[49] Trained in medicine, art, and rhythmic gymnastics, Mensendieck had a holistic approach to understanding the functional and aesthetic elements of the human body and aimed to make her method of cultivating a healthy body accessible to all women. Her *Physical Culture of the Woman* (1906) provided both text and many images of nude girls and women exercising, and thus rendered visible and easily accessible her vision of the modern woman as freed from the cumbersome artifices of nineteenth-century clothing and the attendant gender limitations (e.g., breathing without a corset). Her ambitions were great, and between 1905 and 1924 she transformed these ideas into a network of schools in over eight European countries and the United States.[50]

Practically oriented rather than a theorist, Mensendieck was nonetheless a vital force during the early twentieth century in terms of reimagining gender roles and, in particular, articulating ways for women to gain greater control over their health and appearance. Although she wrote and taught about these issues from the perspective of science rather than politics, her message represented a strong unapologetic feminist voice that found a large following for generations to come.[51] Her writings and schools influenced both the development of the nudist movements in Germany and physical education and modern dance in Europe and North America more broadly.

By emphasizing significant evolutionary differences between men and women like other contemporary feminists, Mensendieck used the eugenicist tropes of the day to advocate for greater attention being paid to women's physical education in relation to the specifics of their physique. In particular, she described the general state of physical well-being of her contemporaries as a devolution of the physical qualities displayed in antiquity and called for a redoubling of efforts to raise young women in better physical conditions. She also described in some detail the types of physical exercises women needed to engage in before and especially after childbirth in order to regain strength and elasticity as an extension of their responsibilities toward themselves and future generations. The nude exercises described in her method were meant to benefit the women themselves, as well as the health of the nation, since healthy, physically fit bodies would translate in better abilities to give birth naturally.[52]

Anarchism

Of the political radical movements that flourished around the turn of the twentieth century and helped galvanize people from many backgrounds toward a complete rebellion against the established political order, anarchism is the closest to being defined through the same words used to identify modernism at the beginning of this book. Anarchists aimed to tear down political, social, cultural, and economic establishments in favor of individual freedom. Individual anarchists and the groups they formed encompassed to various degrees all aspects of human interaction and implicitly, oppression, as embodied in their contemporary world. Some veered more toward labor activism and communism, at least in their critique of capitalism.[53] Others focused more directly on the political privileges of the haves or on the nationalism that drove modern states to war. Yet others, like Emma Goldman, focused on multiple critiques at the same time, and included concerns with gender inequality at the core of her preoccupations.[54]

The arguments for and against identifying anarchism and the actions and publications of individual anarchist leaders, like Goldman, as a modernist, are ongoing, especially since the publication of Allan Antliff's *Anarchist Modernism. Art, Politics, and the First American Avant-Garde* (2001).[55] Some have argued that the aesthetics of *Mother Earth*, the monthly magazine Goldman edited between 1907 and 1915, shows a lack of interest in modernist aesthetics and experimentation in form of expression, even with a few remarkable exceptions in the mix.[56] Others point toward her interest in Nietzsche and especially the inspiration toward radical questioning of the modern condition that she found in his writings as evidence that Goldman was a modernist.[57]

Goldman's *Mother Earth* adopted an aesthetic that was less about radical experimentation and abstraction and more about directness and clarity. But this choice does not necessarily imply that Goldman herself was uninterested in modernism. The publication was one of Goldman's instruments for communicating anarchist ideas with a broad base. Reading her pieces in the journal, one can observe that she aimed at clarity above poetic license or experimentation with words. In short, she seemed more utilitarian than aestheticizing in her mode of expression. In *Mother Earth,* the medium was not the message.

Mother Earth presented a more provocative aesthetic message on the cover of the magazine. In most issues the cover looked unexceptional. But, on occasion, artists like Man Ray contributed with provocative illustrations of the journal's ideas. Better known for his highly staged photographs from the 1920s, Man Ray was a regular contributor to this journal and participant in anarchist circles in the United States. His covers for *Mother Earth*, both the one featured on the next page and the one from the first issue after the beginning of the First World War (August 1914), communicate in dramatic terms the antiwar position of the journal. The radical reimagining of the stars into shots being fired, of the stripes into prison uniforms, and of the flag pole into a crucifix recasts the meaning of the flag, and by extension patriotism/nationalism, into a symbol of warmongering and self-righteousness that have nothing to do with the common good. Man Ray's cover also challenges the gendered trope of wartime heroism as a prerogative of men in uniform: the soldiers in uniform appear like puppets in a staged performance, while the two prisoners featured on the right and bottom parts of the image communicate powerlessness and even emasculation.

Goldman herself provided an abundance of commentaries that challenged the gender norms of the day, starting with an article in the first issue of *Mother Earth*, "The Tragedy of Woman's Emancipation."[58] For the author, the liberation of humanity was inextricably tied to reimagining gender roles. And

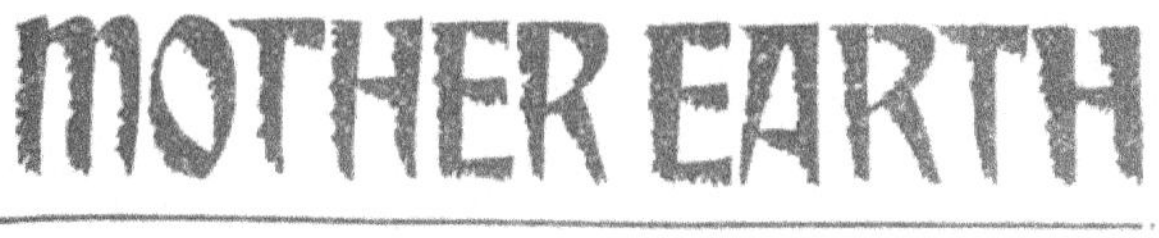

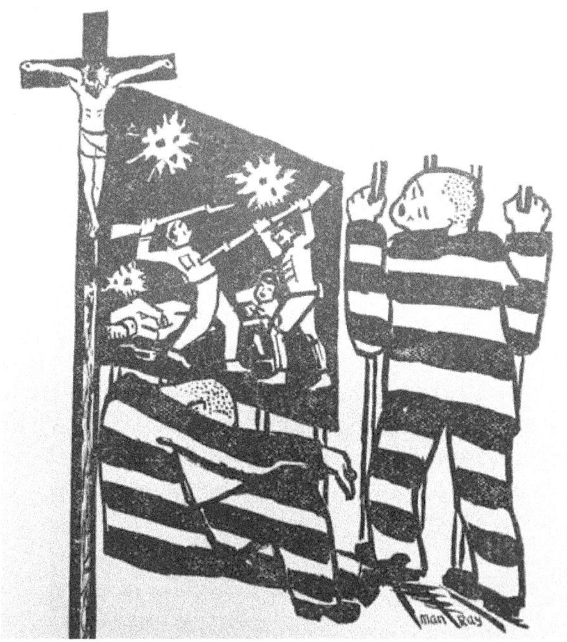

FIGURE 7 *Cover page,* Mother Earth 9, *no. 7 (September 1914).*

though she criticized current practices and laws regarding women's economic power, educational opportunities, and political rights, she also spoke critically of the suffrage movement as something that did not get at the real problem underlying gender relations at the turn of the twentieth century:

> A true conception of the relation of the sexes will not admit of conqueror and conquered; it knows of but one great thing: to give of one's self boundlessly in order to find oneself richer, deeper, better. That alone can fill the emptiness and replace the tragedy of woman's emancipation with joy, limitless joy.[59]

In essence, Goldman laid out a dream of a generous partnership based on freedom and love rather than competitiveness as the foundation for modern gender roles. This vision has been identified by some as romantic and resonant with nineteenth-century ideas about femininity and love, rather than as a modernist idea.[60]

Yet Goldman offered this vision of love within the larger context of accepting modernity, rather than rejecting it. She did not plead for a return to tilling the earth or a rejection of the city as a symbol of modernity and filth. Her sights were set upon women fully participating in public life, no longer pressured by the gender norms of the day and unwilling to simply sign on to the latest trends as a means to be accepted by others:

[Woman's] development, her freedom, her independence, must come from and through herself. First, by asserting herself as a personality, and not as a sex commodity. Second, by refusing the right to anyone over her body; by refusing to bear children, unless she wants them; by refusing to be a servant to God, the State, society, the husband, the family, etc., by making her life simpler, but deeper and richer. That is, by trying to learn the meaning and substance of life in all its complexities, by freeing herself from the fear of public opinion and public condemnation. Only that, and not the ballot, will set woman free, will make her a force hitherto unknown in the world, a force for real love, for peace, for harmony; a force of divine fire, of life-giving; a creator of free men and women.[61]

The radicalness of this vision of gender roles rested in its very simplicity and totality, which shed all sociopolitical constructions as false gods. Goldman invited women to dare articulate other roles for themselves as autonomous individuals, rather than through others' eyes in their upbringing, education, cultural norms, etc. In its place, Goldman cast the free woman as a creator and force of divine fire.

Though Goldman's ideas and aesthetic preferences have led some scholars to consider her a critic of modernism, many of her contemporaries saw a modernist spirit in her and collaborated with her or featured her writing and ideas prominently in their own modernist publications. Margaret Anderson, in *The Little Review*, wrote admiringly about Goldman's ideas and especially her energy and charisma in the public talks she did on her well-attended tours around the country. Anderson placed Goldman alongside the likes of Stein and Elsa von Freytag-Loringhoven, as one of the most remarkable personalities who were shaping the landscape of ideas and especially challenging contemporary gender norms.[62]

Goldman's indomitable energies and radical feminism played a key role in shaping anarchism in the United States before the First World War. Through her personal insistence and the support she found among other men and women in the movement, as well as fellow travelers such as Margaret Sanger and other prominent modernist feminists mentioned here already, the anarchist movement became an important avenue for engaging in debates about and proposals for reshaping gender roles and access to birth control. If Goldman's immediate role in this movement ended with her deportation after the war, the legacy she left behind proved enduring and played an important role for subsequent generations of feminists, especially starting in the 1960s.[63]

To fully appreciate the role played by Goldman in the United States, one can compare it with the development of the anarchist movement in France, especially into the interwar period. A recent analysis by Richard Sonn contends that French anarchism was dominated by a very different attitude toward gender roles, in part fed by general negative attitudes toward feminism on the part of both the leadership of various anarchist factions and by the sexism of fellow travelers such as Breton's circle of surrealists.[64] To be sure, French anarchists focused on issues of individual sexual freedom and control over one's reproductive potential. Some of them, like Jeanne Humbert, advocated for women's unrestricted access to birth control.[65] Yet most other French anarchists, both prior to the interwar period and into the 1920s, regarded women and feminism with suspicion, depicting them as less than rational and thus unable to assume full partnership with men in the quest for individual liberation from the current socioeconomic predicament.[66]

In interwar France, one of the foremost advocates of birth control from a feminist anarchist perspective was Victor Margueritte, already mentioned in this book as part of the modernist canon through his best-seller about the New Woman, *La Garçonne*. Radicalized by the negative reaction of the cultural establishment to that book, Margueritte reached out to Jeanne Humbert for help with research for a book he wanted to write about the debates on birth control in contemporary France from a decidedly pro-abortion stance.[67] The result was another best-seller, entitled *Your Body is Yours* (1927).[68] In addition to its anarcho-feminist approach to depicting women's oppression in modern society, the book provided important practical references to guide women who sought to educate themselves about birth control. It sold over 180,000 copies. Yet despite Margueritte's personal success, the pro-abortion views he espoused and presented publicly many times throughout the 1920s and 1930s did not receive enthusiastic support among French anarchists or their fellow traveler surrealists. Abortion did not become legal in France until 1975.

Communism[69]

The star of anarchism faded gradually during the interwar period partly due to the rise of communism, especially after 1917, as another ideology committed to a radical critique of capitalism and to doing away with the bourgeois state, most prominently in Russia. Communist ideas had contributed to political, social, and aesthetic movements since 1848, but my focus is strictly on the sorts of ideas and policies put forth starting in the late nineteenth century and into the interwar period, that displayed a modernist sensibility and commented directly on gender norms in relation to the new sociopolitical order imagined by communists in the aftermath of the withering away of the bourgeois state.[70]

As with anarchists, communist thinkers, politicians, and artists offered a range of perspectives on gender norms, and this brief survey cannot account for all varieties representative for this period of time. Instead, I will focus on several important examples of communist thinkers who engaged with gender roles. I compare their approach with the writings and actions of the more numerous group of communist leaders whose ideas about gender norms never integrated their critique of the bourgeoisie with critiques of women's specific oppression within bourgeois society.[71] The latter group ended up being the dominant voice into the 1930s and remained so until Marxist feminism developed as a separate movement in the 1960s.[72]

The most important early text tackling the structural historical connection between capitalism and women's oppression is August Bebel's landmark work, *Woman and Socialism* (1879).[73] By equating modern society and capitalism with patriarchy, Bebel made an impassioned and comprehensive argument about the intertwined struggle of the oppressed—workers against bourgeois oppression and women against patriarchal oppression:

> The complete emancipation of woman, and her establishment of equal rights with man is one of the aims of our cultured development, whose realization no power on earth can prevent. But it can be accomplished only by means of a transformation that will abolish the rule of man over man, including the rule of the capitalist over the laborer. Then only can humanity attain its fullest development. The "golden age" of which men have been dreaming, and for which they have been yearning for thousands of years, will come at last. Class rule will forever be at an end, and with it the rule of man over woman.[74]

Bebel's criticism of the gendered nature of class oppression came close to the sentiments Emma Goldman expressed a decade later in her anarchist speeches and writings. Yet Bebel's insistence on identifying women with motherhood as a "natural" function of that gender fell short of the radicalism presented by Goldman and other anarcho-feminists of her day. Bebel was simply a man of his time in this regard.[75]

Still, Bebel's analysis was extremely popular and influential in drawing attention to the oppression of women by men through the legal restrictions over property, primogeniture, inheritance, and marriage. It energized radical leaders like Clara Zetkin, who passionately pressed for continued focus on gender oppression, even as she foregrounded her credentials as a good communist at every turn.[76] Still, as Geoff Eley and others have shown, overall the communist movement was not particularly friendly to "the woman question" both during Bebel's time and throughout the twentieth century, despite claims to the contrary. Many communist and socialist leaders regarded feminist movements as too narrowly bourgeois and, more importantly, women as lacking the abilities to become trustworthy partners. Overall, Marx had little to say about women's oppression in relation to gender norms, and preferred to focus on class conflict without any regard for the question of the gendered aspects of property ownership. Many of his followers chose to ignore gender issues even after Bebel's book sold hundreds of thousands of copies.

Many modernist producers of culture embraced or flirted with anarchism prior to and during the First World War (e.g., Man Ray, Hugo Ball, Tristan Tzara), but reoriented their loyalties toward communism after the war.[77] Those, like the surrealist circle around Breton, chose to support communism in part because of the success of the Bolshevik forces in Russia. The rise of the Leninist concept of "vanguard of the proletariat," as outlined in Lenin's *What is to Be Done?* (1902), presented a radical doctrine of mobilization for those who wanted to remake the world through ideas and to lead the way toward a mass movement that would implement such ideas—the avant-garde.[78] A fearless elite would be called to give birth to the new order, and that is precisely what many modernists saw themselves participating in.

Furthermore, Lenin made it clear numerous times that the vanguard could afford to pay scant attention to gender issues, as their role was to instigate and imbue the proletariat (men and women) with class consciousness above and beyond any other issue. The role he painted for this vanguard was one that people like Breton, for instance, found appealing, as it spoke to his own desire for leadership, as well as to his sexist view of who possessed an enlightened view of the modern condition.[79]

Other prominent modernists who embraced Marxism developed more complex views of gender roles, among them Berthold Brecht. Brecht became a Marxist early on and created a large number of female characters, whom scholars have both celebrated and critiqued as portrayals of gender norms in relation to his critique of capitalism.[80] From his large body of work, on the issue of engaging critically with traditional gender norms, one important and challenging work remains *The Good Person from Szechwan*, a play Brecht began to sketch in the late 1920s but completed in 1943, while in exile from Germany.[81]

The play presents the struggle between good and evil as a parable and comedy, centered around a female character who switches gender and personality back and forth several times. Some feminists have criticized the play as sexist, given the gendered clichés about rationality, emotionality, generosity, weakness, cleverness, and other human characteristics that the central character embodies.[82] Yet other scholars have provided a more nuanced reading of the play from the prism of its function as a parable and comedy. As Alisa Solomon has persuasively demonstrated, the use of gendered clichés in the parable is meant to denaturalize the sexist assumptions behind these clichés rather celebrate them, to generate discomfort and self-criticism on the part of the audience in terms of the kinds of reactions the main character provokes in us.[83]

While the play does not point toward solutions for eliminating the gendered aspects of class oppression, it certainly sheds important insights into the social conditions that give rise to women's specific oppression as a social category. When the main character expresses frustration with the choices she must make between marriage or prostitution, she expresses a critique similar to that presented by Bebel half a century earlier. Later, when she speaks about her dream for freedom as the same as her dream of being alone, without a man (including her masculine alter ego), the main character exposes the duplicity of the contemporary mores regarding morality and gender: though depicted as "good," she cannot be free and act fully as a good person while society rewards only men's wily choices as legitimate. Brecht was no feminist in his own life, to be sure. Yet his modernist Marxism included a lifelong concern with gender roles and in particular with women's oppression by the patriarchal socioeconomic order.

Examples and challenges from inside the communist movement in favor of a specific revolution in gender roles did surface after 1917. None was as forceful and ultimately unsuccessful as Aleksandra Kollontai's. A woman of the elite, Kollontai found herself profoundly unhappy in her wifely predicament next to her officer husband, and at age twenty-five left him to become a revolutionary in St. Petersburg. Anarchism had strong roots in that city, but Kollontai gravitated toward Marxism, especially after she read *Woman and Socialism*. Having embraced communism via Bebel's critique of capitalist gender norms, Kollontai never left concerns with gender inequality behind.

Kollontai did not identify as a feminist, and in fact strenuously critiqued the feminist movements of the nineteenth century as self-defeating and short-sighted, since they did not interrogate the class antagonisms that structurally framed women's oppression at the hand of men under capitalism. Unlike most others who fell short of pointing the way forward for women beyond the critique of capitalism, Kollontai presented the sexually emancipated communist woman as the ideal toward which women should aspire, if they wanted to be freed from oppression and empowered as autonomous individuals:

But whereas with the women of the working class, the struggle for the assertion of their rights, the strengthening of their personality, coincides with the interest of the class, the women of other social strata run into unexpected obstacles: the ideology of their class is hostile to the transformation of the feminine type. . . . For the working class the accomplishment of its mission does not require that she be handmaid of the husband, an impersonal domestic creature, endowed with passive, feminine traits. Rather, it requires a personality rising and rebelling against every kind of slavery, an active conscious equal member of the community, of the class.[84]

More than any other voice in the communist movement and later communist regimes, Kollontai fashioned herself as a revolutionary on behalf of gender norms. Having rejected marriage and compulsory motherhood, Kollontai led the charge in the 1917 antiwar International Women's Day demonstrations that helped radicalize the revolutionary forces, leading to the Bolshevik takeover by November of that year.

Once the Bolsheviks came to power, Kollontai helped develop and for a short time led the women's section of the Communist Party (Zhenotdel), which began to establish policies and programs to supplant many of the domestic caretaking chores that had been the root of women's oppression in bourgeois society.[85] As envisioned by Kollontai, the goal of the Zhenotdel was to eliminate all obstacles against women becoming productive participants of society as well as individuals freed from the shackles of their bourgeois oppression, in this case, marriage, household chores, and motherhood. Crèches, cafeterias, communal apartments and communes, and a factory floor that welcomed women with open arms were all on the agenda of what the communist regime needed to provide for modern women as emancipated workers.

Yet Kollontai's uncompromising insistence on the withering away of marriage and the bourgeois nuclear family as an initial step needed to mobilize women on behalf of communism, and her insistence on equal wages encountered a great deal of criticism from the male leadership of the party. Kollontai was above reproach in her loyalty to the Bolsheviks, but as a singular uncomfortable voice on the matter of gender norms, she was soon removed from the center of decision making. After 1922 she spent most of her remaining years living abroad as ambassador to Norway, and then Mexico and Sweden. She continued to write uncompromising critiques of sexism, but she no longer had influence on shaping gender policies. After 1929, Joseph Stalin decided that women had been liberated and the Zhenotdel was closed down. With that swift termination, the communist regime experiments of the interwar period with radically altering gender norms ended.

Fascism

The literature on the relationship between fascism and modernism has been growing over the past two decades, and I will not rehearse the various arguments presented there regarding fascism as a modernist political movement, as defined through its mobilization-driven, organicist vision of a society organized in a corporatist fashion.[86] In this section, I turn toward the following questions: Did fascism radically reimagine gender norms and how? What changes did fascist regimes promote to enact these new ideas? And to what extent did these ideas for change align with aspects of fascism that other scholars have defined as modernist? Few historians in the crowded field of scholarship on fascism have drawn direct connections between the modernism of fascist ideas and programs, on the one hand, and the specific articulations of gender norms inside this ideology and political regimes or movements linked to it, on the other hand.[87] So it is an important question to continue to investigate, given the radical total transformation of society and the state that the maximalist fascist project imagined.

Concerns with the crisis of masculinity were at the core of the initial appeal of fascism. This is not surprising, given the origins of fascist ideas during the war, based on the specific experiences of men in uniform in both Italy and Germany.[88] Even in places like Romania and Hungary, fascism grew out of frustrations with the outcomes of the First World War from the perspective of men who saw their expectations blasted away (Hungary) or radically bolstered (Romania) by the postwar order. In Italy, for instance, we see modernist aesthetics and a concern with how men should be treated and viewed as a formative force in the development of fascism. From the first events initiated in Fiume by the founder of the movement, the modernist poet Gabriele d'Annunzio, the uniforms, salute, marches, and other visual displays of gendered performance helped communicate the specific ideas that animated fascism. Virility was a central value espoused by the fascists, to be emulated by men and even women, to some extent.[89] The rhetoric employed by people like Hitler and Mussolini focused on reaching back toward purer times to reassert the sort of strength fascists believed the nineteenth-century liberal order had slowly eliminated from society. Among them were physical strength, heterosexual prowess, leadership in familial matters, and the courage to sacrifice one's life on the battlefield to protect the nation.

Yet other elements crucial to defining masculinity under fascism were new and show a modernist bent: it wasn't sufficient for men to aspire to the qualities listed above; under the strict control of the state, they needed to mobilize their natural potential in these areas and suppress other tendencies in the interest of the nation.[90] The social hierarchy advocated by fascists was also new, even as it invoked traditions: the racist and xenophobic aspects of this order were articulated through science arguments about the health of the nation and its future, rather than by appealing to tradition. For instance, eugenicist ideas about crime, alcoholism, and syphilis framed much of the discussion about what sorts of men would be the future leaders of the nation and which ones would be the dangerous population.[91]

Nobody was able to build as successful an aesthetic that focused on the gendered modernist aspects of fascism as Leni Riefenstahl. Her innovations as a filmmaker dovetailed with her ambitions to coax this art form into a tool for molding revolutionary new representations of power and gender roles. Courted by Hitler after he saw her first feature movie, *The Blue Light* (1932), Riefenstahl ended up producing the most famous Nazi movie, *The Triumph of the Will* (1935), billed as a documentary. Many critics consider the film, however, as a more complex blend of both documentary and propaganda material: in essence, Riefenstahl imposed her own vision of masculinity, and her own understanding of Hitler, in particular, on crafting images she herself controlled very carefully during the shooting process and then edited. As one scholar recently concluded, Riefenstahl in effect helped construct the most iconically referenced (and sometimes ironically referenced, as in the case of *The Great Dictator*) images of Hitler as leader of a mass virile movement of male bodies.[92]

Fascist definitions of femininity were secondary and followed the primary anchoring of gender roles around concerns with masculinity, even in Riefenstahl's own representation in *Triumph of the Will*. The fascists who deployed eugenicist ideas sometimes went so far as to focus on the important ways in which women needed to be mobilized, most often as the genetic intergenerational carrier responsible for ensuring that both their bodies and those they brought into the world were healthy. Thus, for some women activists, the arrival of fascism as a regime (Italy) or the rise of a fascist movement (e.g., Great Britain) presented opportunities to increase their participation in the public arena. In Italy, for instance, whose budding liberal constitutional monarchy had never reached so far as to include women, fascism seemed to present new opportunities for participating actively in society and being valued publicly for what many still identified as their main gender roles—as dutiful wives and daughters.[93] We see a similar reaction in Romania, where a number of women joined the movement in the 1930s as a way to fulfill what they viewed as their primary social roles—their potential as wives and mothers.[94]

Be that as it may, there are important differences in the way women's roles were being imaged by comparison with men's: women were to remain passive, secondary, subservient to the new fascist men, rather than become their partners or competitors. If supporters of eugenics did sometimes use these theories to advocate for women's empowerment through control over birthing practices (e.g., Marie Stopes), no fascist thinkers, artists, or political leaders offered any such versions of how women's biological destiny should be mobilized for the greater good. Fascism remained a movement dominated by men and concerns with masculinity, with women playing the role of supporters at best and objects at worst.

* * *

This incursion into several areas of scientific, political, and cultural modernism has served as an invitation to imagine a richer array of manifestations that produced important departures from established gender norms starting in the late nineteenth century in Europe and North America. My aim has been to suggest enhancing the modernist canon through the prism of experimentation with gender roles as a fundamental aspect of how these rebellious innovators engaged with politics, art, writing, or scientific discourse.

I am not equating experimentation with a progressive agenda, since the radical changes proposed by some of these innovators were antidemocratic at best, and totalitarian antihumanist at worse. However, it is important to recognize the explosive implications of these attempts to refashion sexual norms, to craft sexual identity, to engage with the crisis of masculinity, and to set out new possibilities for women to engage in social and political activities, in all of their forms, be they democratizing, empowering, or on the contrary, authoritarian and limiting. The vocabulary for thinking about what masculinity and femininity imply in the twentieth century came about through these experimentations.

Ultimately, whether or not the actual politics and aesthetics of any of these specific modernists were meant to open up more possibilities for individuals to imagine themselves as gendered beings, the long-term effect of these ideas and cultural products has been to in fact diversify our definitions of gender roles. The sexual spectrum imagined by Hirschfield at the turn of the century was critiqued and selectively used by the Nazis when they came to power, yet the ideas he helped generate have continued to play a role in how people thought about sexual identity into the second half of the twentieth century. For instance, the work of Alfred Kinsey from the 1930s and into the 1950s was tributary to the important discursive departures Hirschfield had introduced decades before.[95] Similarly, though Kollontai's gender radicalism was rejected by her own radical left-wing movement, the solutions she envisioned for ending patriarchal oppression are now part of mainstream feminist thinking about gender roles.

Conclusion

This brief survey of the modernist canon and analysis of lesser-known figures and movements that sought to reshape aesthetics, politics, and societies between the late nineteenth century and the beginning of the Second World War has brought into sharper focus if and how modernism engaged with established gender norms. Starting from a feminist humanist perspective on how we understand change over time, I have suggested rethinking how we define the extent of rebelliousness and innovation that self-avowed modernists brought to cultural production and politics. My aim has been to situate our analysis of modernism in a deeper cultural and political context that accounts not just for formal experimentation, but also for the networks of power and broader social norms against which modernists articulated their rebellion.

My analysis joins the scholarship of the last decade in mainstreaming gender analysis in the research on, writing about, and curating modernism. Major museums, publishing endeavors, and retrospective exhibits continue to relegate gendered aspects of modernism to marginal references, footnotes, and bibliographies, at best. Yet we cannot fully appreciate either the contribution of these innovators to changing the cultural and political landscape or the complexity of individual works, if we continue to think about modernist engagements with gender norms as somehow secondary to their core questions and critiques of the established order.

The first part of this book has offered examples of how gender analysis enhances this understanding and adds important nuances to our appreciation for and critique of some of the most prominent names in the modernist canon, from Ibsen to Picasso, from Wilde to Woolf. My intention here has been to walk through a familiar landscape of works and personalities with a new perspective and examine the claims to innovation and departure from the establishment in terms of assumptions about gender norms and representation of gender roles in the ideas, activities, and works of these self-avowed modernists. My point has been not to reject the claim to originality made by these producers of culture, which has been reaffirmed by the critics who anointed them as part of the modernist canon. Rather, I wish to render our comprehension of these contributions more nuanced and more closely connected to a holistic understanding of historical change, which includes both appreciation and also criticism, as warranted by historical evidence of challenges to gender roles.

In the second part of this study I turned my attention to three important sets of contexts that are necessary for understanding how the modernist canon came about. In particular, I examined how gender regimes created institutional and discursive frameworks of power inequality between men and women, as well as between heteronormativity and alternative sexual identities. By following several examples of individuals whose activities were innovative in both a broad cultural sense and specifically in challenging some of these gender structural inequalities, I explained how these activities became erased out of histories of modernism. I also argued for the need to reconsider that erasure: the boldness of their vision and the radicalness of their rebellion need to be considered in relation to the distance between the limitations faced by those modernists by virtue of their gender, such as lack of access to art education and opportunities to exhibit with prestigious Salons, or interdictions for married women to work in certain professions, and these modernists' activities.

The three contexts that help us better understand the impact of gender norms on modernist activities and the subsequent construction of the modernist canon are: (1) educational/professional training opportunities; (2) the collecting of and selling modernist products; and (3) writing about and curating modernism. Fundamentally, the institutions that helped train producers of culture were subject to the same two-tiered, sexist institutional limitations present in the political and social establishments more broadly. If women were restricted by legal, economic, and cultural norms that men never had to consider, then the distance they traveled from those strictures toward new forms of expressing creativity is far greater than men had to consider. Modernist women's rebellion exposed them to greater risks socially and culturally and therefore should be regarded as such, and not just by simply reading the words they wrote or examining the artifacts they produced.

Modernist artifacts and actions were constructed into a canon through a process of filtering at the hands of collectors and critics. In particular, the work done by women collectors has been poorly integrated into our understanding of how the modernist canon emerged. My analysis picks up on recent work done by several feminist scholars to suggest that looking at the gendered aspects of these activities helps us better understand how much we owe the beginnings of modernist art collections, galleries, and museums to women collectors.

Finally, I turned toward the impact that scholars and curators have had on framing our understanding of modernism. In particular, I pointed out the unevenness of gender considerations in this literature. The scholarship itself was initially subject to the same discursive limitations that made it more difficult for women to become artists and writers. Though challenges to the sexist assumptions embedded in how art history and criticism were written rose from the beginnings of the modernist movement itself, it was not until the 1970s that we see the modernist canon begin to be seriously questioned by feminist scholars.

In the third part of this study I extended my field of inquiry to suggest that a number of scientific and political movements that rose during the period covered here should be considered more thoroughly as part of the modernist canon, because of the radicalness of the changes they wanted to bring to gender norms. In short, I see the field of gender norms as an area of modernist experimentation that is broad, comprehensive, and potentially explosive, so much so that we cannot regard it as somehow secondary to painting, writing, or theater. What Emma Goldman wished to bring about was in essence far more radical and all encompassing than anything expressed by the surrealist manifestoes of the 1920s. That Goldman has not been a recurrent presence in the modernist canon but André Breton is should give us pause about what our gendered assumptions are regarding what is radical and innovative—what is core to modernism.

*   *   *

My call for an enhanced modernist canon with gender roles as a core element of analysis is also a critique of the contemporary trends in the commodification of modernism as an artifact of mass consumption. With the rise of a global market for art objects, and with tourism to Europe and North America encompassing a much broader array of people from across the world, cities that celebrate their modernist sites are facing new challenges in terms of communicating what is impressive, worth seeing, and also worth buying in relation to the modernist canon. There are the art objects themselves, whose value keeps going up, except when disenchanted collectors or family members decide to offload sizable collections.[1] There is a self-fulfilling prophecy in how the art market works, with the best-known names always fetching more because of the "brand" recognition. Marie Laurencin does not fetch as much as Pablo Picasso, despite the much larger body of work and unevenness of the individual pieces produced by Picasso.

For those who cannot afford to acquire original modernist artifacts, there are ample opportunities for collecting experiences in museums and exhibits, as well as objects that have a modernist aesthetic or copies of famous modernist pieces. One can purchase Klimt *Kiss* umbrellas, Frida Kahlo postcards, Picasso totes, and any number of other consumable tchotchkes of various sizes and prices at any one of many museums with a modernist collection. Fashion designers have long used elements of modernist art, bringing new interpretations, as well as renewed visibility to some artists.

Pop music has also been a venue for reinterpreting and using modernism for mass consumption. During the early days of MTV, Madonna's tune "Express Yourself" became one of the most viewed music videos. It was a tribute to *Metropolis*, rearticulated from a feminist stance, with the singer cast as the powerful central figure, based on the female robot in the film.

The intense and multifaceted commodification of modernism as "style" rather than content has created its own challenges to altering the modernist canon. There are far more options for anyone to express a critique or appreciative tribute, but the audiences for such reinterpretations are hard to engage across already established preferences. As consumers, people tend to gravitate toward the familiar and the pleasure fulfilling, rather than the strange and disturbing, unless one finds pleasure or satisfaction in engaging with the strange and disturbing. Educational experiences, such as attending an exhibit, become framed more by what is already likely to capture and retain the attention of the public, rather than critical examinations that push against the gender norms and assumptions of the viewers themselves. And with the commodification of museums in relation to what is sold in the gift shops and not just what is on view there, the visitor can have an experience that simply confirms expectations and the familiar, rather than being taken on a journey of uncomfortable discovery and challenges to gender norms. The commodification of modernism thus beckons us to continue the search for making gender analysis an important component of how we construct the interpretive framework of the canon.

Notes

Prologue

1 For more information on the museum, see http://www.musee-magritte-museum.be/Portail/Site/Typo3.asp?lang=FR&id=languagedetect (accessed March 10, 2015).

2 The work is a five-piece ensemble of canvases that depicts parts of Magritte's wife's body: face, breasts, torso and vagina, upper legs, and lower legs and feet. The female body is thus rendered as an assemblage of parts, with primary emphasis on sexuality, as the canvases depicting the breasts and vagina are the largest and most centrally located parts of the ensemble, drawing the viewer's eye to these elements, rather than the eyes or facial expression of Georgette. The reification of women's sexuality is also underscored by the title. "Eternal" can be defined also as "essential" or "universal." Georgette's humanity is reduced thus to "evidence" of essential qualities of femininity—the material proof of a concept, rather than an individual whose body parts are neither eternal nor mere evidence.

3 René Magritte, "Réponse à l'enquête SUR LA CRISE DE LA PEINTURE," in *René Magritte*, ed. André Blavier (Paris: Flammarion, 2001), 85.

4 *La Révolution Surréaliste* 5, no. 12 (1929): 73.

5 Raymond Williams, *The Politics of Modernism: Against the New Conformists* (New York: Verso, 1989).

Introduction: What Sort of Rebellion?

1 Williams, *The Politics of Modernism*.

2 Eugene Lunn, *Marxism and Modernism: An Historical Study of Lukács, Brecht, Benjamin, and Adorno* (Berkeley: University of California Press, 1982), 12.

3 Ibid., quoted from Marianne DeKoven, *Rich and Strange: Gender, History, Modernism* (Princeton: Princeton University Press, 1991).

4 See, for instance, Christopher Butler, *Modernism: A Very Short Introduction* (Oxford: Oxford University Press, 2010).

5 See, for instance, Marilyn S. Kushner, Kimberly Orcutt, and Casey Nelson Blake, *The Armory Show at 100: Modernism and Revolution* (New York: New York Historical Society, 2013).

6 While music is an important area of the modernist movement, I only focus on cabaret as a type of (sometime) musical performance engaged with gender norms.

7 See, for instance, David James (ed.), *The Legacies of Modernism: Historicising Postwar and Contemporary Fiction* (Cambridge: Cambridge University Press, 2011); Ulrike Knöfel, "The Legacy of Modernism: Celebrating 90 Years of Bauhaus," *Spiegel International*, February 27, 2009, at http://www.spiegel.de/international/zeitgeist/the-legacy-of-modernism-celebrating-90-years-of-bauhaus-a-610283.html (accessed March 10, 2015).

8 Marshall Berman, *All That Is Solid Melts Into Air: The Experience Of Modernity*, 9th edn (New York: Verso, 2009), 345–46.

9 Ibid., 15–16.

10 Rita Felski, *The Gender of Modernity* (Cambridge, MA: Harvard University Press, 1995), 2–3.

11 Roger Griffin, *Modernism and Fascism: The Sense of a Beginning under Mussolini and Hitler* (Basingstoke: Palgrave Macmillan, 2007); Peter Fritzsche, *A Nation of Fliers German Aviation and the Popular Imagination* (Cambridge, MA: Harvard University Press, 1992).

12 Griffin, *Modernism,* 62.

13 Marius Turda, *Modernism and Eugenics* (Basingstoke: Palgrave, 2010), 2.

14 Although Turda's volume excels in many regards, it does not consider the gendered implications of eugenics as an important theme, despite the author's acknowledgment that the control of reproductive functions is a core element of this intellectual and social movement.

15 Raymond Williams, "When Was Modernism," in *Politics of Modernism*, 31–35.

16 William A. Johnsen, "Madame Bovary: Romanticism, Modernism, and Bourgeois Style," *MLN* 94, no. 4 (1979): 843–50.

17 More on this topic in Chapter 3.

18 Virginia Woolf, *A Room of One's Own* (New York: Harcourt Brace & Co., 1989).

19 Milton W. Brown, *The Story of the Armory Show*, 2nd edn (New York: Abbeville Press, 1988); Milton W. Brown, *American Painting from the Armory Show to the Depression* (Princeton: Princeton University Press, 1955). For an example of the staying power of his scholarship, see Paul S. Boyer and Melvyn Dubofsky (eds.), *The Oxford Companion to United States History* (Oxford: Oxford University Press, 2001).

20 Brown, *Story of the Armory Show*, 59. For a more detailed critique of this issue, see: Shelley Staples, "'The Part Played By Women': The Gender of Modernism at the Armory Show," at http://xroads.virginia.edu/~museum/armory/gender.html (accessed October 19, 2016); Jennifer Pfeifer Shircliff,

"Women of the 1913 Armory Show: Their Contributions to the Development of American Modern Art," PhD diss., University of Louisville, Louisville, 2014.

21 Boyer and Dubofsky, *Oxford Companion*, 577.

22 For an excellent overview of the impact of feminist scholarship on art history, see Griselda Pollock, "Women, Art, and Art History: Gender and Feminist Analyses," in *Oxford Bibliographies*, at http://www.oxfordbibliographies.com/view/document/obo-9780199920105/obo-9780199920105-0034.xml (accessed March 10, 2015). Her analysis identifies Joan Kelly-Gadol, "Did Women Have a Renaissance?," in *Becoming Visible: Women in European History*, eds. Renate Bridenthal and Claudia Koonz (Boston: Houghton Mifflin, 1977), 19–50 and Linda Nochlin, "Why Have There Been No Great Women Artists?," in *Women, Art and Power and Other Essays* (New York: Westview Press, 1988 [1971]), 147–58 as the two foundational texts for making women artists visible in art historiography. For the literary canon, Susan Gubar and Sandra Gilbert provoked a similar shift in criticism and historiography with Sandra M. Gilbert and Susan Gubar, *The Madwoman in the Attic the Woman Writer and the Nineteenth-Century Literary Imagination* (New Haven: Yale University Press, 1979); Felski, *The Gender of Modernity*.

23 Michel Foucault, *The History of Sexuality. Vol. 1: An Introduction* (London: Allen Lane, 1978); Joan W. Scott, "Gender: A Useful Category of Historical Analysis," *The American Historical Review* 91, no. 5 (1986): 1053–75.

24 From the very long list of studies relevant here, I include a small selection: Bonnie Kime Scott and Mary Lynn Broe (eds.), *The Gender of Modernism: A Critical Anthology* (Bloomington: Indiana University Press, 1990). Jayne E. Marek, *Women Editing Modernism: "Little" Magazines & Literary History* (Lexington: University Press of Kentucky, 1995); Elizabeth Jane Harrison and Shirley Peterson (eds.), *Unmanning Modernism: Gendered Re-Readings* (Knoxville: University of Tennessee Press, 1997); Lisa Rado (ed.), *Modernism, Gender, and Culture: A Cultural Studies Approach* (New York: Garland, 1997); Katy Deepwell (ed.), *Women Artists and Modernism* (Manchester: Manchester University Press, 1998); Susan Stanford Friedman, *Mappings: Feminism and the Cultural Geographies of Encounter* (Princeton: Princeton University Press, 1998); Gillian Perry (ed.), *Gender and Art* (New Haven: Yale University Press, 1999); Bonnie Kime Scott (ed.), *Gender in Modernism: New Geographies, Complex Intersections* (Urbana: University of Illinois Press, 2007); and Geetha Ramanathan, *Locating Gender in Modernism: The Outsider Female* (New York: Routledge, 2012).

25 See, for instance, Perry, *Gender and Art*; Gerald N. Izenberg, *Modernism and Masculinity: Mann, Wedekind, Kandinsky through World War I* (Chicago: University of Chicago Press, 2000).

26 A search through the journal's archives in April 2015 showed 140 articles that engage with questions about masculinity, by contrast with 112 dealing with femininity. There are 562 articles that make mention of "gender," almost 300 of them dealing with men in some fashion, and almost 400 with women.

27 Judith Butler, *Gender Trouble: Feminism and the Subversion of Identity* (New York: Routledge, 2006).

28 See, for instance, Nadine Hubbs, *The Queer Composition of America's Sound: Gay Modernists, American Music, and National Identity* (Berkeley: University of California Press, 2004).

29 Charles Musser, "1913: A Feminist Moment in the Arts," in *The Armory Show at 100*, ed. Kushner, Orcutt, and Blake, 169–79.

30 Shircliff, "Women of the 1913 Armory Show."

31 The journal came out twice a year until 2015, when it started to come out three times a year, signaling an increased interest in and production of studies dedicated to understanding modernism. It is a publication of the British Association for Modernist Studies.

32 The number of occurrences is even more impressive when looking at the total number of research articles published in each issue, which range between five and eight, with an average of seven. Thus, out of 133 articles that have come out, almost half make reference to women's issues, and more than a quarter discuss gender. In short, every issue engages with questions of gender.

Chapter 1 Modernism before the Great War

1 Leila J. Rupp, *Worlds of Women: The Making of an International Women's Movement* (Princeton: Princeton University Press, 1997); Oliver Janz and Daniel Schönpflug (eds.), *Gender History in a Transnational Perspective: Networks, Biographies, Gender Orders* (New York: Berghahn, 2014).

2 See, for instance, Nathaniel D. Wood, *Becoming Metropolitan: Urban Selfhood and the Making of Modern Cracow* (DeKalb: Northern Illinois University Press, 2010); Peter Fritzsche, *Reading Berlin 1900* (Cambridge, MA: Harvard University Press, 1998).

3 Morag Shiach (ed.), *The Cambridge Companion to the Modernist Novel* (Cambridge: Cambridge University Press, 2007).

4 On *Madame Bovary*, see Laurence M. Porter (ed.), *A Gustave Flaubert Encyclopedia* (Westport: Greenwood Press, 2001); on *Awakenings*, see Elizabeth Nolan and Janet Beer (eds.), *Kate Chopin's The Awakening: A Sourcebook* (London: Routledge, 2004); on *A Doll's House*, see James Walter McFarlane (ed.), *The Cambridge Companion to Ibsen* (Cambridge: Cambridge University Press, 1994).

5 Einar Ingvald Haugen, *Ibsen's Drama: Author to Audience* (Minneapolis: University of Minnesota Press, 1979), 10.

6 Beth Holmgren, *Starring Madame Modjeska: On Tour in Poland and America* (Bloomington: Indiana University Press, 2012), 289.

7 Carole Pateman, *The Sexual Contract* (Stanford: Stanford University Press, 1988). Great Britain saw important changes in married women's property rights starting in the 1870s.

8 Maria Bucur, "The Economics of Citizenship: Gender Regimes and Property Rights in Romania in the 20th Century," in *Gender and Citizenship in Historical and Transnational Perspective*, eds. Anne Epstein and Rachel Fuchs (Basingstoke: Palgrave, 2017), 143–65.

9 Henrik Ibsen, *A Doll's House* (Clayton: Prestwick House, 2006), 76.

10 Emma Goldman, "The Social Significance of Henrik Ibsen," *The Social Significance of the Modern Drama* (Boston: Richard G. Badger, 1914), 11–12.

11 In the United States, from the beginning of the nineteenth century, a variety of state laws made provisions in different parts of the country for women to control their own property and have full legal autonomy. See Kathleen S. Sullivan, *Constitutional Context: Women and Rights Discourse in Nineteenth-Century America* (Baltimore: Johns Hopkins University Press, 2007).

12 Oscar Wilde, *The Uncensored Picture of Dorian Gray*, ed. Nicholas Frankel (Cambridge: Belknap Press, 2011).

13 Margaret Cruikshank, *The Gay and Lesbian Liberation Movement. Revolutionary Thought/Radical Movements* (New York: Routledge, 1992), 65.

14 Oscar Wilde, *The Picture of Dorian Gray* (New York: Charterhouse Press, 1904), 114 and 323.

15 Crispin Sartwell, "Art for Art's Sake," in *Encyclopedia of Aesthetics*. 4 vols, ed. Michael Kelly (Oxford: Oxford University Press, 1998), vol. 1, 118–20.

16 Petra Dierkes-Thrun, *Salomé's Modernity: Oscar Wilde and the Aesthetics of Transgression* (Ann Arbor: University of Michigan Press, 2011).

17 Sucheta Mazumdar, Vasant Kaiwar, and Thierry Labica (eds.), *From Orientalism to Postcolonialism: Asia-Europe and the Lineages of Difference* (London: Routledge, 2011).

18 Rita Severi, "Oscar Wilde, La Femme Fatale and the Salomé Myth," in *Proceedings of the Xth Congress of the International Comparative Literature Association*, eds. Anna Balakian and James Wilhelm (New York: Garland, 1985), 458.

19 Oscar Wilde, *Salomé* (London: John Lane, 1907).

20 Brad Bucknell, "On 'Seeing' Salomé," *ELH* 60, no. 2 (1993): 503–26.

21 Alon Rachamimov, "The Disruptive Comforts of Drag: (Trans)Gender Performances among Prisoners of War in Russia, 1914–1920," *The American Historical Review* 111, no. 2 (2006): 362–82.

22 Bucknell, "On 'Seeing,'" 519.

23 Rachamimov, "Disruptive Comforts."

24 Julian Young, *Friedrich Nietzsche: A Philosophical Biography* (Cambridge: Cambridge University Press, 2010).

25 Sigmund Freud, *The Interpretation of Dreams* (New York: Basic Books, 2010).

26 Luis A. Cordón, *Freud's World: An Encyclopedia of His Life and Times* (Santa Barbara: Greenwood, 2012), 467.

27 B. J. Cohler and R. M. Galatzer-Levy, "Freud, Anna, and the Problem of Female Sexuality," *Psychoanalytic Inquiry* 28 (2008): 3–26; Thomas Walter Laqueur, *Making Sex: Body and Gender from the Greeks to Freud* (Cambridge, MA: Harvard University Press, 1990).

28 Juliet Mitchell and Sangay K. Mishra, *Psychoanalysis and Feminism: A Radical Reassessment of Freudian Psychoanalysis*, 2nd rev. edn (New York: Basic Books, 2000).

29 Richard von Krafft-Ebing, *Psychopathia Sexualis. Eine Klinisch-Forensische Studie* (Stuttgart: Verlag von Ferdinand Enke, 1886).

30 Turda, *Modernism and Eugenics.*

31 Harry Oosterhuis, "Sexual Modernity in the Works of Richard von Krafft-Ebing and Albert Moll," *Medical History* 56, no. 2 (2012): 133–55.

32 Alexandra Minna Stern, "Gender and Sexuality: A Global Tour and Compass," in *The Oxford Handbook of the History of Eugenics*, eds. Alison Bashford and Philippa Levine (Oxford: Oxford University Press, 2010), 173–91.

33 Kimberly A. Smith, *Between Ruin and Renewal: Egon Schiele's Landscapes* (New Haven: Yale University Press, 2004), 48.

34 Jan Cavanaugh, *Out Looking in: Early Modern Polish Art, 1890-1918* (Berkeley: University of California Press, 2000).

35 The paintings were almost destroyed after completion, but Klimt was able to repurchase them when the university refused to exhibit the paintings. *Jurisprudence* changed hands several times and was eventually destroyed at the end of the Second World War as part of a Nazi cache of stolen art from Austria after the Anschluss.

36 Carl E. Schorske, *Fin-de-Siècle Vienna: Politics and Culture* (New York: Vintage Books, 1981).

37 Ibid.

38 Jill Scott, "Public Debates and Private Jokes in Gustav Klimt's The Kiss: Effeminate Aestheticism, Virile Masculinity, or Both?," in *Gender and Modernity in Central Europe: The Austro-Hungarian Monarchy and Its Legacy*, ed. Agata Schwartz (Ottawa: University of Ottawa Press, 2010), 29–46.

39 William Rubin, Helene Seckel, and Judith Cousins, *Les Demoiselles d'Avignon* (New York: The Museum of Modern Art, 1995).

40 Patricia Leighten, "The White Peril and *L'Art nègre*: Picasso, Primitivism, and Anticolonialism," *The Art Bulletin* 72, no. 4 (1990): 609–30.

41 Rubin, Seckel, and Cousins, *Les Demoiselles.*

42 For a critical view of the claim that Brâncuşi had a Platonic style, see Anna Chave, *Constantin Brâncuşi: Shifting the Bases of Art* (New Haven: Yale University Press, 1993).

43 Ibid.

44 The name of the piece has been translated both as *The Endless Column* and *The Column of the Infinite.*

45 *"Mărgele"* in Romanian.

46 Sanda Miller, "Brâncuşi's 'Column of the Infinite,'" *The Burlington Magazine* 122, no. 928 (1980): 470–80.

47 Eric Shanes, *Constantin Brâncuşi* (New York: Abbeville Press, 1989), 97.

48 *"Coloana recunoștinței fără sfârșit,"* in Romanian.

49 Brâncuşi returned to the theme of the *Kiss* numerous times, but the first work to bear this name was completed in 1907.

50 For instance, there is not a single cross present in the ensemble, the symbol used most frequently in Romanian Christian Orthodox memorials, inclusive of those from the First World War. See Maria Bucur, *Heroes and Victims: Remembering War in Twentieth-Century Romania* (Bloomington: Indiana University Press, 2009).

51 Nicola Shaughnessy, *Gertrude Stein* (Tavistock: Northcote/British Council, 2007).

52 The best example of this style is her *Tender Buttons. Objects—Foods— Rooms* (1914), which featured collage-like fragments such as: "Please pale hot, please cover rose, please acre in the red stranger, please butter all the beef-steak with regular feel faces." The attributes of her writing most often included repetition, incongruity, and syntax that defied grammar rules and logic. See http://www.gutenberg.org/files/15396/15396-h/15396-h.htm (accessed October 14, 2016).

53 Gertrude Stein, *Three Lives* (New York: Vintage Books, 1958). Her first piece of fiction, "Q.E.D.," was a coming-out story about her becoming a lesbian, but it remained unpublished until after the author's death. It was released as *Things As They Are, A Novel in Three Parts by Gertrude Stein, Written in 1903 but Now Published for the First Time* (Pawlet: Banyan Press, 1950).

54 Jonathan L. Goldman, *Modernism Is the Literature of Celebrity* (Austin: University of Texas Press, 2012), 93.

55 Barbara Will, *Gertrude Stein, Modernism, and the Problem of "Genius"* (Edinburgh: Edinburgh University Press, 2000), 62. Otto Weininger's theories were apparently particularly influential for Stein: Otto Weininger, *Sex and Character* (New York: G. P. Putnam's Sons, 1906).

56 The show traveled afterwards to Chicago and Boston.

57 Kushner, Orcutt, and Blake, *The Armory Show at 100.*

58 In Kushner, Orcutt, and Blake, *The Armory Show at 100*, the large volume commemorating the centenary of the Armory Show, only six women artists' works from the exhibit are featured.

59 Allan Antliff, *Anarchist Modernism: Art, Politics, and the First American Avant-Garde* (Chicago: University of Chicago Press, 2001).

60 Kushner, Orcutt, and Blake, *The Armory Show at 100*, 171.

61 William B Scott and Peter M Rutkoff, *New York Modern: The Arts and the City* (Baltimore: Johns Hopkins University Press, 1999), 113.

62 Marian Wardle (ed.), *American Women Modernists. The Legacy of Robert Henri, 1910-1945* (Provo: Brigham Young University Museum of Art; New Brunswick: Rutgers University Press, 2005).

63 Shircliff, "Women of the 1913 Armory Show."

64 I am simply describing practices as they occurred at the time. Whether the male artists were somehow generous in their gestures rather than embarrassed, self-interested, or simply conscious of the privileges they had vis-à-vis women artists is a different issue, which I discuss more directly in the second part of this study.

Chapter 2 Modernism Flourishes

1 Christopher M. Clark, *Sleepwalkers: How Europe Went to War in 1914* (New York: Harper Perennial, 2014).

2 Susan R. Grayzel, *Women's Identities at War: Gender, Motherhood, and Politics in Britain and France during the First World War* (Chapel Hill: University of North Carolina Press, 1999).

3 Maria Bucur, "Between the Mother of the Wounded and the Virgin from Jiu. Romanian Women and the Gender of Heroism during the Great War," *Journal of Women's History* 12, no. 2 (2000): 30–56.

4 Maureen Perrie (ed.), *The Cambridge History of Russia. Vol. 2, Imperial Russia, 1689-1917* (Cambridge and New York: Cambridge University Press, 2006.)

5 Maria Bucur, "Women's Stories as Sites of Memory: Remembering Romania's World Wars," in *Gender and War in Twentieth Century Eastern Europe*, eds. Nancy M. Wingfield and Maria Bucur (Bloomington: Indiana University Press, 2006), 171–92.

6 Louise Miller, *A Fine Brother: The Life of Captain Flora Sandes* (London: Alma Books, 2014).

7 Bucur, "Between the Mother of the Wounded."

8 Laurie Stoff, *They Fought for the Motherland: Russia's Women Soldiers in World War I and the Revolution* (Lawrence: University Press of Kansas: 2006).

9 Bucur, *Heroes and Victims*.

10 Karen L. Levenback, *Virginia Woolf and the Great War* (Syracuse: Syracuse University Press, 1999), 114–15.

11 Paul Fussell, *The Great War and Modern Memory* (New York: Oxford University Press, 2000).

12 Siegfried Sassoon, *The War Poems of Siegfried Sassoon* ([S.l.]: Merchant Books, 2009), 49.

13 Daniel J. Sherman, *The Construction of Memory in Interwar France* (Chicago and London: University of Chicago Press, 1999).

14 Denis Rolland, *La Grève Des Tranchées: Les Mutineries de 1917* (Paris: Imago, 2005).

15 The silence about these issues continues today. In the recently launched *International Encyclopedia of the First World War*, which features prominent historians with a great deal of research and accolades under their belt, this issue of women war volunteers' invisibility does not even get a mention, while there are multiple mentions of the support given to war widows in places like Australia or India. See http://encyclopedia.1914-1918-online.net/home (accessed December 17, 2015).

16 See, for instance, David Richard Sonn, *Sex, Violence, and the Avant-Garde: Anarchism in Interwar France* (University Park: Pennsylvania State University Press, 2010).

17 For left-wing movements, see Geoff Eley, *Forging Democracy the History of the Left in Europe, 1850-2000* (Oxford: Oxford University Press, 2002); for the right, see Kevin Passmore (ed.), *Women, Gender, and Fascism in Europe, 1919-45* (New Brunswick: Manchester University Press, 2003).

18 Pericles Lewis (ed.), *The Cambridge Companion to European Modernism*. Cambridge Companions to Topics (Cambridge: Cambridge University Press, 2011), 205.

19 Georg Schmidt (ed.), *Sophie Taeuber-Arp* (Basel: Holbein Verlag, 1948), 125.

20 Louise R. Noun, *Three Berlin artists of the Weimar Era: Hannah Höch, Käthe Kollwitz, Jeanne Mammen* (Des Moines: Des Moines Art Center, 1994), 21.

21 According to one source, the first Höch solo retrospective exhibit took place in 1973 in Paris and then traveled to Berlin: http://weimarart.blogspot.com/2010/08/hannah-hoch-brushflurlets-and-beer.html (accessed March 11, 2015). More recently, in 2014 the Whitechapel Gallery organized the first major retrospective of the artist in the UK: http://www.whitechapelgallery.org/about/press/hannah-hoch (accessed March 11, 2015).

22 She eventually became Salvador Dali's lover and model.

23 Other interpretations for the choice of who appears in the painting point toward the prefiguration of surrealism and Ernst's interest in "hermetic knowledge." M. E. Warlick, *Max Ernst and Alchemy: A Magician in Search of Myth* (Austin: University of Texas Press, 2001), 66–68.

24 André Breton, *Manifestoes of Surrealism* (Ann Arbor: University of Michigan Press, 1969).

25 Ibid., 3.

26 Susan Rubin Suleiman, *Subversive Intent: Gender, Politics, and the Avant-Garde* (Cambridge, MA: Harvard University Press, 2012).

27 As quoted in Sonn, *Sex, Violence, and the Avant-Garde*, 77.

28 *La Révolution Surréaliste* 5, no. 12 (1929): 73.

29 Alice Gambrell, *Women Intellectuals, Modernism, and Difference. Transatlantic Culture, 1919–1949* (New York: Cambridge University Press, 1997).

30 Ibid., 49.

31 Tace Hedrick, *Mestizo Modernism. Race, Nation, and Identity in Latin American Culture, 1900-1940* (New Brunswick: Rutgers University Press, 2003).

32 Ibid.

33 Gambrell, *Women Intellectuals*, chapter two.

34 Andreas Huyssen, *After the Great Divide: Modernism, Mass Culture, Postmodernism* (Bloomington: Indiana University Press, 1986); Michael Minden and Holger Bachmann, *Fritz Lang's "Metropolis." Cinematic Views of Technology and Fear* (Columbia and Woodbridge: Camden House; Boydell & Brewer, 2002).

35 R. L. Rutsky, "The Mediation of Technology and Gender: Metropolis, Nazism, Modernism," *New German Critique* 60 (1993): 3–32.

36 Barbara Kosta, *Willing Seduction: The Blue Angel, Marlene Dietrich, and Mass Culture* (New York: Berghahn Books, 2009).

37 John A. Williams, "*The Blue Angel (Der Blaue Engel)* by Josef von Sternberg," *Modernism/modernity* 20, no. 4 (2013): 801–04.

38 In 1919 Kollwitz became the first woman elected to the Prussian Academy of Arts.

39 This choice was based on both ideological considerations, as Kollwitz was a lifelong supporter of the socialist cause, as well as financial ones, since her membership in the Prussian Academy of Arts provided her with a stipend that enabled Kollwitz to have a comfortable life regardless of the financial rewards of selling her art.

40 Eva Martin Sartori and Dorothy Wynne Zimmerman (eds.), *French Women Writers: A Bio-Bibliographical Source Book* (New York: Greenwood Press, 1991), 563.

41 Virginia Woolf, *Night and Day* (London: Duckworth, 1919).

42 Virginia Woolf, *A Room of One's Own* (New York: Harcourt Brace & Co., 1989 [1929]).

43 Leonard V. Smith, *The Embattled Self. French Soldiers' Testimony of the Great War* (Ithaca: Cornell University Press, 2007).

44 Andrew Lawrence Roberts, *From Good King Wenceslas to the Good Soldier Švejk a Dictionary of Czech Popular Culture* (Budapest: Central European University Press, 2005).

45 For an analysis of Chaplin's modernism, see Saverio Giovacchini, *Hollywood Modernism: Film and Politics in the Age of the New Deal* (Philadelphia: Temple University Press, 2001), chapter four; and Susan McCabe, *Cinematic Modernism Modernist Poetry and Film* (Cambridge: Cambridge University Press, 2009), chapter two.

46 Peter Jelavich, *Berlin Cabaret* (Cambridge, MA: Harvard University Press, 1993); Harold B. Segel, *Turn-of-the-Century Cabaret. Paris, Barcelona, Berlin, Munich, Vienna, Cracow, Moscow, St. Petersburg, Zurich* (New York: Columbia University Press, 1987).

47 Patrice Petro, *Joyless Streets: Women and Melodramatic Representation in Weimar Germany* (Princeton: Princeton University Press, 1989).

48 Klaus Theweleit, *Male Fantasies* (Minneapolis: University of Minnesota Press, 1987).

49 On the impact of cabaret culture on the work of modernist artists, see Andrew Stephenson, "'New Ways of Modern Bohemia': Edward Burra in London, Paris, Marseilles and Harlem," *Tate Papers*, no. 19 (2013), available at http://www.tate.org.uk/research/publications/tate-papers/new-ways-modern-bohemia-edward-burra-london-paris-marseilles-and#footnote95_ia9zw3b (accessed March 12, 2015).

50 Carole Sweeney, *From Fetish to Subject. Race, Modernism, and Primitivism, 1919-1935* (Westport: Praeger Publishers, 2004), chapter two.

51 Baker attempted to engage with the racist culture in the United States, but returned to Europe disappointed and humiliated. See Matthew Pratt Guterl, *Josephine Baker and the Rainbow Tribe* (Cambridge, MA: Harvard University Press, 2014).

52 Sieglinde Lemke, *Primitivist Modernism. Black Culture and the Origins of Transatlantic Modernism* (Oxford: Oxford University Press, 1998), 110. See also Julie Townsend, "Un-fixing Baker. Against a Criticism of Stasis," *Modernist Cultures* 9, no. 1 (2014): 62–70.

53 George Orwell, *Homage to Catalonia* (London: Secker and Warburg, 1938).

54 Lisa Margaret Lines, *Milicianas. Women in Combat in the Spanish Civil War* (Lanham: Lexington Books, 2012).

Chapter 3 The Modernist Canon: How Did it Come About?

1 See, for instance, the work of Susan Gubar, Sandra Gilbert, or Bonnie Kime Scott, for older critiques: Sandra M. Gilbert and Susan Gubar (eds.), *The Female Imagination and the Modernist Aesthetic* (New York: Gordon and Breach Science Publishers, 1986); Bonnie Kime Scott and Mary Lynn Broe (eds.), *The Gender of Modernism: A Critical Anthology* (Bloomington: Indiana University Press, 1990). For more recent critiques, see Geetha Ramanathan, *Locating Gender in Modernism: The Outsider Female* (New York: Routledge, 2012).

2 Nikolaus Pevsner, *Academies of Art. Past and Present* (London: Cambridge University Press, 1940).

3 One exception was the Haarlem Guild of St. Luke, which began admitting women in 1631. Judith Leyster, whose work is featured in the National Gallery in Washington, DC, was one prominent member of this guild. She had a prodigious career and trained a number of artists herself, but became lesser known over time, as Franz Hals, also a member of her guild, gained notoriety, to the point of having her work identified as Franz Hals's. See Cornelis Hofstede de Groot, "Judith Leyster," *Jahrbuch der Königlich Preussischen Kunstsammlungen* 14 (1893): 190–98; and Elke Linda Buchholz, *Women Artists*, translated by Stephen Telfer (Munich, London, and New York: Prestel, 2003).

4 One important element of control on the part of art guilds was allowing its members to use their own signature on their works, once the apprentices moved from initiation to mastery. Without the right to signature, an artist could not display or sell her work through established venues, at least not as her own. This regulation rendered many women artists invisible for posterity.

5 Wendy Wassying Roworth (ed.), *Angelica Kauffman. A Continental Artist in Georgian England* (London: Reaktion Books, 1992).

6 This date relates to the establishment of the School in its modern form, though the institution it evolved from was founded in 1648 as the French Academy for Painting and Sculpture.

7 Gabriel P. Weisberg and Jane R. Becker (eds.), *Overcoming All Obstacles. The Women of the Académie Julian* (New York and New Brunswick: Dahesh Museum; Rutgers University Press, 1999).

8 George Marcu (ed.), *Dicţionarul personalităţilor feminine din România* (Bucharest: Editura Meronia, 2009).

9 Cecilia Cuţescu-Storck, *Fresca unei vie i* (Bucovina: Editura Torou iu, 1943).

10 Her appointment as the first woman on the faculty of the School of Fine Arts was in the department of decorative arts. At that time she worked in two media—oil on canvas, and mural painting. Neither technique falls into the traditional definition of "decorative." Still, this is how her work is characterized in descriptions of the museum dedicated to her and her husband's work. See, for instance, http://www.dozadebine.ro/bucuresti-muzeul-de-arta-plastica-frederic-storck-si-cecilia-cutescu-storck (accessed March 12, 2015).

11 For Yugoslavia, see Marina Vujnović, "Forging the Bubikopf Nation: A Feminist Political-Economic Analysis of *Ženski List*, Interwar Croatia's Women's magazine, for the Construction of an Alternative Vision of Modernity," PhD diss., University of Iowa, Iowa City, 2009; for Poland, see Helena Goscilo and Beth Holmgren (eds.), *Poles Apart. Women in Modern Polish Culture* (Bloomington: Slavica Publishers, 2006).

12 Marevna, *Life in Two Worlds: A True Chronicle of the Origins of Montparnasse* (London: Abelard-Schuman, 1962), 183. See also Perry, *Gender and Art*.

13 Weisberg and Becker, *Overcoming All Obstacles*; Anthea Callen, *Women Artists of the Arts and Crafts Movement, 1870-1914* (New York: Pantheon Books, 1979).

14 Callen, *Women Artists*; Pevsner, *Academies of Art*.

15 Martin P. Eidelberg, *A New Light on Tiffany. Clara Driscoll and the Tiffany Girls* (London: New York Historical Society, 2007).

16 Judy Attfield and Pat Kirkham (eds.), *A View From the Interior. Feminism, Women and Design* (London: The Women's Press, 1989).

17 For an excellent analysis of working conditions for women at that time, see Eileen Boris, *Home to Work. Motherhood and the Politics of Industrial Homework in the United States* (Cambridge: Cambridge University Press, 1994).

18 Frederick J. Hoffman, Charles Allen, and Carolyn F. Ulrich, *The Little Magazine. A History and a Bibliography* (Princeton: Princeton University Press, 1946).

19 For a critique of the approach to analyzing the work of women editors in Hoffman, Allen, and Ulrich, *The Little Magazine*, see Marek, *Women Editing Modernism*.

20 Anderson was the founding editor, but in 1916 she brought on board Jane Heap, at that time Anderson's lover, as a coeditor. Heap was also a writer. Heap and Anderson's partnership on the journal (1916–29) outlasted their personal intimacy. In 1917, Ezra Pound, who acted as the foreign editor in London, joined the two. Pound played a crucial role in bringing James Joyce's *Ulysses* to *The Little Review* for serial publication, and has subsequently been more widely known as an editor of the journal than Anderson and Heap, even though his work on bringing out the *Review* was in no way more central than that of the other two editors. See Marek, *Women Editing Modernism*, 9.

21 Hoffman, Allen, and Ulrich, *The Little Magazine*, 52.

22 Suzanne W. Churchill and Adam McKible (eds.), *Little Magazines & Modernism. New Approaches* (Aldershot: Ashgate, 2007).

23 The issue in question was September 1916. It featured thirteen blank pages at the beginning, with the explanation: "*The Little Review* hopes to become a magazine of Art. The September issue is offered as a Want Ad." The blank pages represented a protest against what were considered weak submissions, as well as a provocative way to uphold the journal's ambitious motto: "Making No Compromise with the Public Taste."

24 Margaret Anderson, "Announcement," *The Little Review* 1, no. 1 (1914): 2.

25 From *Züricher Post*, May 7, 1916, as quoted in Josh MacPhee and Erik Ruin (eds.), *Realizing the Impossible. Art Against Authority* (Oakland: AK Press, 2007), 275.

26 Susan Jones, *Literature, Modernism, and Dance* (Oxford: Oxford University Press, 2013), chapter two.

27 Janet C. Bishop, Cécile Debray, and Rebecca A. Rabinow (eds.), *The Steins Collect. Matisse, Picasso, and the Parisian Avant-Garde* (New Haven: Yale University Press, 2011).

28 A recent book identifies Sarah Stein as an important, though long-ignored, force among the three in terms of her specific tastes and appetite for modernist art. Even Matisse commented admiringly on her exquisite sensibilities. Other scholars speak of Leo being the initial and most important force in developing the collection, at least at the beginning. For my purposes here, it is more important to note that all three Steins put their individual imprint on the collection that emerged and was eventually dispersed. Charlotte Gere, *Great Women Collectors* (London; New York: Harry N. Abrams, 1999), 147–50.

29 Lucy Jane Daniel, *Gertrude Stein* (London: Reaktion Books, 2009), 137–38.

30 Shircliff, "Women of the 1913 Armory Show," 101.

31 Gere, *Great Women Collectors*, 150–55.

32 Mary V. Dearborn, *Mistress of Modernism. The Life of Peggy Guggenheim* (Boston: Houghton Mifflin, 2004).

33 It is entirely possible that similar developments were taking place in England, France, Germany, Poland, etc., but the initial research in the archives of museums and art collections has not been done to the extent it has grown in regard to the United States, so my comments here are restricted to the most thoroughly researched case study. It poses an interesting research and comparative history set of questions, and I hope this book generates further interest in this topic.

34 Shircliff, "Women of the 1913 Armory Show," chapter three.

35 Davidge was the fundraiser who convinced eighteen of the twenty-four donors to provide funds for the show. Until very recently, her name was not properly acknowledged as the most important individual behind this effort. Ibid., 49.

36 Ibid., 46.

37 To fully appreciate the actual worth of these financial contributions, the value of the dollar in 1913 was twenty-five times smaller than it is today. Thus, a $1,000 donation at that time would be the equivalent of $25,000 today.

38 Shircliff, "Women of the 1913 Armory Show," chapter three.

39 Gere, *Great Women Collectors*, 150–55.

40 Mark A. Swiencicki, "Consuming Brotherhood. Men's Culture, Style and Recreation as Consumer Culture, 1880-1930," in *Consumer Society in American History. A Reader*, ed. Lawrence B. Glickman (Ithaca: Cornell University Press, 1999), 207–40.

41 Dianne Sachko Macleod, *Enchanted Lives, Enchanted Objects. American Women Collectors and the Making of Culture, 1800-1940* (Berkeley: University of California Press, 2008).

42 Shircliff, "Women of the 1913 Armory Show," 115–16.

43 Ibid., 90–91.

44 Ibid., 60–61.

45 Women both loaned to the Armory Show and purchased works that were on sale there.

46 In addition to the derogatory treatment of women in Brown's *Story of the Armory Show*, see also Walt Kuhn, *The Story of the Armory Show* (New York: Self-published, 1938); for a critique of this approach, see Shircliff, "Women of the 1913 Armory Show," introduction.

47 Ibid.

48 Shircliff, "Women of the 1913 Armory Show"; Gere, *Great Women Collectors*, 170–73.

49 http://www.moma.org/about/history (accessed February 27, 2015). The relevant page is difficult to find from the home page, another indicator that the museum's curators and publicity team are not focused on making this history prominently visible and broadly known.

50 Shircliff, "Women of the 1913 Armory Show," chapter three.

51 In addition to purchasing through the Steins, after Leo and Gertrude parted ways and their collection was fragmented, the Cone sisters continued to build their collection by buying some of those items. Many of them are on display today at the Baltimore Museum of Art.

52 See http://beinecke.library.yale.edu/collections/highlights/katherine-s-dreier-papers-société-anonyme-archive (accessed March 12, 2015).

53 Duncan Phillips, *The Eye of Duncan Phillips: A Collection in the Making* (Washington, DC: Phillips Collection in association with Yale University New Haven, 1999).

54 Duncan Phillips, *A Collection in the Making. A Survey of the Problems Involved in Collecting Pictures, Together with Brief Estimates of the Painters in the Phillips Memorial Gallery* (Washington, DC: E. Weyhe, 1926).

55 Phillips, *Collection in the Making*, 66.

56 Francis M. Naumann, "'An Explosion in a Shingle Factory': Marcel Duchamp's *Nude Descending a Staircase (No. 2)*," in *The Armory Show at 100*, eds. Kushner, Orcutt, and Blake, 203–09.

57 Pam Meecham and Julie Sheldon, *Modern Art. A Critical Introduction* (London: Routledge, 2005), chapter four.

58 Musser, "1913: A Feminist Moment," in *The Armory Show at 100*, eds. Kushner, Orcutt, and Blake, 178.

59 Shircliff, "Women of the 1913 Armory Show," 146.

60 The concept of "white slavery" has received renewed criticism more recently. See Barbara Antoniazzi, *The Wayward Woman: Progressivism, Prostitution, and Performance in the United States, 1888-1917* (Madison: Fairleigh Dickinson. 2014).

61 It was executed in plaster for the show and subsequently thought lost until the 1970s, when a collector was able to piece together the plaster model and execute a bronze version of the sculpture.

62 Louise Noun, *Abastenia St. Leger Eberle, Sculptor (1878-1942)* (Des Moines: Des Moines Art Center, 1980).

63 Ibid., 14.

64 Ibid., 9.

65 Robin Walz, *Modernism*, 2nd edn (Abingdon: Routledge, 2013), chapter nine.

66 Griselda Pollock, *Avant-Garde Gambits, 1888-1893. Gender and the Color of Art History* (New York: Thames and Hudson, 1993).

67 Walz, *Modernism*; Felski, *Gender of Modernity*.

68 An illustrative example is the website and additional materials on offer at the MoMA website dedicated to education. A search of the word "gender" brings up the following page: http://www.moma.org/learn/moma_learning/

themes/investigating-identity/constructing-gender (accessed March 12, 2015). The page includes a Powerpoint presentation and several illustrations, most of them of works that date from the 1970s and onward. Overall, the narrative suggests that challenges to gender norms came with the feminist movement of the 1960s and 1970s, leaving the question of the gender innovations of the modernists active in the 1900s to the 1940s largely obscured. The only inkling we get about the contributions from that period is the following sentence: "In the first half of the twentieth century, artists such as Claude Cahun and Frida Kahlo made self-portraits that emphasize the fluidity of gender, refusing to adhere to statically masculine or feminine characteristics." However, the historiography on literary modernism has been more responsive to including gender as a core framework of analysis. See Marianne DeKoven, "Modernism and Gender," in *The Cambridge Companion to Modernism*, ed. Michael Levenson (Cambridge: Cambridge University Press, 1999), 174–93.

69 Bonnie Kime Scott and Mary Lynn Broe (eds.), *The Gender of Modernism. A Critical Anthology* (Bloomington: Indiana University Press, 1990).

70 Churchill and McKible, *Little Magazines & Modernism*; Felski, *Gender of Modernity*.

Chapter 4 A New Set of Criteria: Rebellion, Rejection, and Reimagining Gender

1 Griffin, *Modernism*, 62.

2 Mary Chapman, *Making Noise, Making News. Suffrage Print Culture and U.S. Modernism* (Oxford and New York: Oxford University Press, 2014); Lisa Tickner, *The Spectacle of Women. Imagery of the Suffrage Campaign, 1907-14* (Chicago: University of Chicago Press, 1988); Christine Stansell, *Feminist Promise* (New York: Random House, 2011); Margaret Mary Finnegan, *Selling Suffrage: Consumer Culture & Votes for Women* (New York: Columbia University Press, 1999).

3 Chapman, *Making Noise*, chapter two.

4 Ibid.

5 "Miss Richardson's Statement," *The Times*, March 11, 1914.

6 The weekly came out between 1918 and 1940.

7 Louise Weiss, *Délivrance* (Paris: Albin Michel, 1936).

8 In 1979 the European Parliament was relatively powerless, as it did not have the authority to pass any legislation that was binding to the member countries.

9 Margaret R. Higonnet, Jane Jenson, Sonya Michel, and Margaret Collins Weitz (eds.), *Behind the Lines. Gender and the Two World Wars* (New Haven: Yale University Press, 1987); Wingfield and Bucur, *Gender and War*.

10 Elizabeth Crawford, *The Women's Suffrage Movement. A Reference Guide, 1866-1928* (London and New York: Routledge, 2001).

11 Ibid. For cases in Eastern Europe, see Passmore, *Women, Gender, and Fascism*.

12 Francisca de Haan, Krasimira Daskalova, and Anna Loutfi (eds.), *Biographical Dictionary of Women's Movements and Feminisms in Central, Eastern, and South Eastern Europe. 19th and 20th Centuries* (Budapest: Central European University Press, 2006).

13 Malgorzata Fidelis, *Women, Communism, and Industrialization in Postwar Poland* (Cambridge: Cambridge University Press, 2014), 39–40.

14 De Haan, Daskalova, and Loutfi, *Biographical Dictionary*, 162–64.

15 Paul Peppis, *Sciences of Modernism: Ethnography, Sexology, and Psychology* (New York: Cambridge University Press, 2014); in the recent *History of Psychology: A Global Perspective*, Eric Shiraev identifies the origins of psychology much earlier in time, but concedes that psychoanalysis originates with the work of Freud, Jung, and Alfred Adler in the mid-1880s. Eric Shiraev, *A History of Psychology. A Global Perspective* (Thousand Oaks: SAGE, 2011).

16 Ibid.

17 Barbara Engler, *Personality Theories* (Belmont: Wadsworth, 2014), 110–34.

18 Before 1900, Switzerland and France were the first countries to allow women admission to medical training schools. Suzanne Le-May Sheffield, *Women and Science. Social Impact and Interaction* (New Brunswick: Rutgers University Press, 2006), 109–10.

19 Nancy Chodorow, *Feminism and Psychoanalytic Theory* (New Haven: Yale University Press, 1989).

20 Harry Oosterhuis, *Stepchildren of Nature. Krafft-Ebing, Psychiatry, and the Making of Sexual Identity* (Chicago: University of Chicago Press, 2000).

21 Robert Beachy, *Gay Berlin. Birthplace of a Modern Identity* (New York: Knopf, 2014).

22 Ibid.

23 Ibid.

24 Ibid.

25 Robert A Peel (ed.), *Marie Stopes, Eugenics and the English Birth Control Movement* (London: Galton Institute, 1997).

26 Marie Carmichael Stopes, *Married Love or Love in Marriage*, Kindle Edition, Kindle Locations, 209–10.

27 Jesse Wolfe, *Bloomsbury, Modernism, and the Reinvention of Intimacy* (Cambridge: Cambridge University Press, 2011), 8.

28 Patricia Anderson, *Passion Lost. Public Sex, Private Desire in the Twentieth Century* (Toronto: Thomas Allen Publishers, 2001), 40.

29 Stopes claimed to have been the first to open such a clinic and sparred publicly with Sanger over this issue, even though they shared a great deal in common. Jean H. Baker, *Margaret Sanger. A Life of Passion* (New York: Hill and Wang, 2011), 171–72.

30 Turda, *Modernism and Eugenics.*

31 Maria Bucur, "Remapping the Historiography of Modernization and State-Building in Southeastern Europe through Hygiene, Health and Eugenics," in *Health, Hygiene and Eugenics in Southeastern Europe to 1945*, eds. Marius Turda, Christian Promitzer, and Sevasti Trubeta (Budapest: Central European University Press, 2011), 427–46; Wendy Kline, *Building a Better Race: Gender, Sexuality, and Eugenics from the Turn of the Century to the Baby Boom* (Berkeley: University of California Press, 2005); Nancy Stepan, *The Hour of Eugenics. Race, Gender, and Nation in Latin America* (Ithaca: Cornell University Press, 1991); Daylanne K. English, *Unnatural Selections. Eugenics in American Modernism and the Harlem Renaissance* (Chapel Hill: University of North Carolina Press, 2004).

32 Maria Bucur, "In Praise of Wellborn Mothers. On Eugenics and Gender Roles in Interwar Romania," *East European Politics and Societies* 9, no. 1 (1995): 123–42.

33 Maria Bucur, "Mişcarea eugenistă şi rolurile de gen," in *Patriarhat şi emancipare în istoria gîndirii politice româneşti*, eds. Maria Bucur and Mihaela Miroiu (Iaşi: Polirom, 2002).

34 Maria Bucur, *Eugenics and Modernization in Interwar Romania* (Pittsburgh: Pittsburgh University Press, 2002).

35 Ibid.; George L. Mosse, *The Image of Man. The Creation of Modern Masculinity* (New York: Oxford University Press, 1996).

36 Bucur, *Eugenics and Modernization.*

37 Maria Bucur, "Fallen Women and Necessary Evils: Eugenicist Cultural Representations of and Legal Battles over Prostitution in Interwar Romania," in *"Blood and Homeland." Eugenics and Racial Nationalism in Central and Southeast Europe, 1900-1940*, eds. Marius Turda and Paul Weindling (Budapest and New York: Central European University Press, 2007), 335–50.

38 Ibid.

39 On Romania, see Bucur, "In Praise"; on India, see Clare Hanson, *Eugenics, Literature, and Culture in Post-War Britain* (New York: Routledge, 2013), 132.

40 Bucur, "In Praise."

41 See above discussion about Stopes.

42 Bucur, *Eugenics and Modernization.*

43 Gisela Bock and Susan James (eds.), *Beyond Equality and Difference. Citizenship, Feminist Politics, and Female Subjectivity* (London and New York: Routledge, 1992).

44 Sarah Toulalan and Kate Fisher (eds.), *The Routledge History of Sex and the Body. 1500 to the Present* (Abingdon: Routledge, 2013), chapter four.

45 Karl Eric Toepfer, *Empire of Ecstasy. Nudity and Movement in German Body Culture, 1910-1935* (Berkeley: University of California Press, 1997), 33–35;

see also Eric D. Weitz, *Weimar Germany. Promise and Tragedy* (Princeton: Princeton University Press, 2007).

46 Toepfer, *Empire of Ecstasy.*

47 Michael Hau, *The Cult of Health and Beauty in Germany. A Social History, 1890-1930* (Chicago: The University of Chicago Press, 2003), 189.

48 Weitz, *Weimar Germany.*

49 Toepfer, *Empire of Ecstasy.*

50 Robin Veder, "Seeing Your Way to Health: The Visual Pedagogy of Bess Mensendieck's Physical Culture System," *International Journal of the History of Sport* 28, nos. 8–9 (2011): 1336–52.

51 Toepfer, *Empire of Ecstasy*, 39–41.

52 Mike Huggins and Mike O'Mahony (eds.), *The Visual in Sport* (London: Routledge, 2014), 252.

53 Allan Antliff, *Anarchist Modernism: Art, Politics, and the First American Avant-Garde* (Chicago: University of Chicago Press, 2001).

54 Ibid.; Alix Kates Shulman, *To the Barricades. The Anarchist Life of Emma Goldman* (New York: Open Road Integrated Media, 2011).

55 For an analysis that considers Goldman as a modernist anarchist, see Antliff, *Anarchist Modernism;* for an analysis that goes to some length to demonstrate she was not, see Kathy E. Ferguson, *Emma Goldman. Political Thinking in the Streets* (Lanham: Rowman & Littlefield Publishers, 2011).

56 Kathy E. Ferguson, "Assemblages of Anarchists: Political Aesthetics in *Mother Earth*," *The Journal of Modern Periodical Studies* 4, no. 2 (2013): 171–94.

57 Anne Fernihough, *Freewomen and Supermen. Edwardian Radicals and Literary Modernism* (Oxford: Oxford University Press, 2013), 60.

58 Emma Goldman, "The Tragedy of Woman's Emancipation," *Mother Earth* 1, no. 1 (1906): 9–18.

59 Ibid., 18.

60 Ferguson, *Emma Goldman.*

61 Emma Goldman, *Anarchism and Other Essays*, at http://theanarchistlibrary. org/library/emma-goldman-anarchism-and-other-essays (accessed March 15, 2015).

62 Margaret Anderson, "The Challenge of Emma Goldman," *The Little Review* 1, no. 3 (March 1914): 5–9.

63 Robert E. Weir, *Workers in America. A Historical Encyclopedia* (Santa Barbara: ABC-CLIO, 2013), 300.

64 Sonn, *Sex, Violence.*

65 Ibid., 122.

66 Ibid.

67 Ibid., 122–23.

68 Victor Margueritte, *Ton corps est à toi* (Paris: Flamarrion, 1927).

69 For the purposes of this brief incursion, I am not differentiating among different varieties of Marxism within the broad spectrum of the left in the twentieth century.

70 Eugene Lunn, *Marxism and Modernism. An Historical Study of Lukács, Brecht, Benjamin, and Adorno* (Berkeley: University of California Press, 1982); Williams, *The Politics of Modernism.*

71 Eley, *Forging Democracy.*

72 See, for instance, Michèle Barrett, *Women's Oppression Today. The Marxist/ Feminist Encounter*, rev. edn (New York: Verso, 1988).

73 Though there is no an extensive analysis of this book as modernist, the book is cited by several scholars either on timelines of modernism or as part of modernist literature. See, for instance, Vassiliki Kolocotroni, Jane Goldman, and Olga Taxidou (eds.), *Modernism: An Anthology of Sources and Documents* (Chicago: University of Chicago Press, 1998), 60–64; Mark S. Micale (ed.), *The Mind of Modernism. Medicine, Psychology, and the Cultural Arts in Europe and America, 1880-1940* (Stanford: Stanford University Press, 2004), 28.

74 August Bebel, *Woman and Socialism* (New York: Labor News Co., 1904), 349.

75 Eley, *Forging Democracy*, 99–100.

76 See especially her interview with V.I. Lenin in 1920. Available at https://www.marxists.org/archive/zetkin/1920/lenin/zetkin1.htm (accessed February 11, 2015).

77 Sonn, *Sex, Violence.*

78 Vladimir I. Lenin, *Essential Works of Lenin. "What Is to Be Done?" And Other Writings*, with an introduction by and Henry M Christman (New York: Dover Publications, 1987).

79 Sonn, *Sex, Violence.*

80 Siegfried Mews (ed.), *A Bertolt Brecht Reference Companion* (Westport: Greenwood Press, 1997); Carol Martin (ed.), *A Sourcebook of Feminist Theatre and Performance. On and beyond the Stage* (London: Routledge, 1996); Simon Shepherd and Mick Wallis, *Drama/Theatre/Performance* (London: Routledge, 2004), 185–89.

81 Bertolt Brecht, *The Good Person of Szechwan* (New York: Penguin Books, 2008).

82 Elizabeth Wright, "*The Good Person from Szechwan*: Discourse of a Masquerade," in *The Cambridge Companion to Brecht*, eds. Peter Thomson and Glendyr Sacks, 2nd edn (Cambridge: Cambridge University Press, 2006), 117–27.

83 Alisa Solomon, *Re-Dressing the Canon. Essays on Theater and Gender* (London: Routledge, 1997).

84 Aleksandra Kollontai, *The Autobiography of Sexually Emancipated Communist Woman*, available at https://www.marxists.org/archive/kollonta/1926/autobiography.htm [1926] (accessed March 15, 2015).

85 Elizabeth A. Wood, *The Baba and the Comrade. Gender and Politics in Revolutionary Russia* (Bloomington: Indiana University Press, 1997).

86 Griffin, *Modernism and Fascism*; Jeffrey Herf, *Reactionary Modernism. Technology, Culture, and Politics in Weimar and the Third Reich* (Cambridge: Cambridge University Press, 1984); Peter Fritzsche, *Germans into Nazis* (Cambridge, MA: Harvard University Press, 1998).

87 Some examples include John Champagne, *Aesthetic Modernism and Masculinity in Fascist Italy* (London: Routledge, 2014); Melanie Hawthorne and Richard Joseph Golsan (eds.), *Gender and Fascism in Modern France* (Hanover: University Press of New England, 1997); Passmore, *Women, Gender*.

88 Griffin, *Fascism and Modernism*; Fritzsche, *Germans into Nazis*.

89 Barbara Spackman, *Fascist Virilities. Rhetoric, Ideology, and Social Fantasy in Italy* (Minneapolis: University of Minnesota Press, 1996).

90 On the modernist aspects of this type of biopolitics, see Turda, *Modernism and Eugenics*.

91 Bucur, *Eugenics and Modernization*.

92 Annalisa Zox-Weaver, *Women Modernists and Fascism: Female Modernists and the Allure of the Dictator* (Cambridge: Cambridge University Press, 2011), 24–56.

93 Passmore, *Women, Gender*.

94 Bucur, "In Praise"; Roland Clark, "Die Damen der Legion: Frauen in rumäischen faschistischen Gruppierungen," in *Inszenierte Gegenmacht von rechts: Die "Legion Erzengel Michael" in Rumänien 1918-1938*, eds. Armin Heinen and O. J. Schmitt (Munich: Oldenberg Verlag, 2013), 193–216.

95 Heike Bauer, "Sexology Backward: Hirschfeld, Kinsey and the Reshaping of Sex Research in the 1950s," in *Queer 1950s: Rethinking Sexuality in the Postwar Era*, eds. Heike Bauer and Matt Cook (Basingstoke: Palgrave Macmillan, 2012), 133–49; available at https://www.academia.edu/1239050/8_Sexology_Backward_Hirschfeld_Kinsey_and_the_Reshaping_of_Sex_Research_in_the_1950s._Heike_Bauer (accessed March 1, 2015).

Conclusion

1 Doreen Carvajal, "Picasso's Granddaughter Plans to Sell Art, Worrying the Market," *New York Times*, February 4, 2015, available at http://www.nytimes.com/2015/02/05/arts/design/picassos-granddaughter-plans-to-sell-art-worrying-the-market.html (accessed March 15, 2015).

Selected Bibliography of Secondary Sources

Anderson, Patricia. *Passion Lost: Public Sex, Private Desire in the Twentieth Century.* Toronto: Thomas Allen Publishers, 2001.

Antliff, Allan. *Anarchist Modernism: Art, Politics, and the First American Avant-Garde.* Chicago: University of Chicago Press, 2001.

Antoniazzi, Barbara. *The Wayward Woman: Progressivism, Prostitution, and Performance in the United States, 1888-1917.* Madison, WI: Fairleigh Dickinson, 2014.

Armstrong, Tim. *Modernism: A Cultural History.* Themes in Twentieth-Century Literature and Culture. Cambridge: Polity, 2005.

Armstrong, Tim. *Modernism, Technology, and the Body: A Cultural Study.* Cambridge: Cambridge University Press, 1998.

Attfield, Judy, and Pat Kirkham, eds. *A View from the Interior: Feminism, Women, and Design.* London: Women's Press, 1989.

Atwood, Kathryn J. *Women Heroes of World War I: 16 Remarkable Resisters, Soldiers, Spies, and Medics.* Chicago: Chicago Review Press, 2014.

Baker, Jean H. *Margaret Sanger: A Life of Passion.* New York: Hill and Wang, 2011.

Barrett, Michèle. *Women's Oppression Today: The Marxist/Feminist Encounter.* Rev. ed. New York: Verso, 1988.

Bashford, Alison, and Philippa Levine, eds. *The Oxford Handbook of the History of Eugenics.* Oxford: Oxford University Press, 2010.

Bauer, Heike. "Sexology Backward: Hirschfeld, Kinsey and the Reshaping of Sex Research in the 1950s," in *Queer 1950s: Rethinking Sexuality in the Postwar Era*, edited by Heike Bauer and Matt Cook, 133–49. Basingstoke, UK: Palgrave Macmillan, 2012.

Beachy, Robert. *Gay Berlin: Birthplace of a Modern Identity.* New York: Knopf, 2014.

Berman, Marshall. *All That Is Solid Melts Into Air: The Experience Of Modernity.* 9th ed. New York: Verso, 2009.

Bishop, Janet C., Cécile Debray, and Rebecca A. Rabinow, eds. *The Steins Collect: Matisse, Picasso, and the Parisian Avant-Garde.* New Haven: Yale University Press, 2011.

Bock, Gisela, and Susan James, eds. *Beyond Equality and Difference: Citizenship, Feminist Politics, and Female Subjectivity.* New York: Routledge, 1992.

Boris, Eileen. *Home to Work. Motherhood and the Politics of Industrial Homework in the United States.* Cambridge: Cambridge University Press, 1994.

Boyer, Paul S., and Melvyn Dubofsky, eds. *The Oxford Companion to United States History*. Oxford: Oxford University Press, 2001.

Brown, Milton W. *American Painting from the Armory Show to the Depression*. Princeton: Princeton University Press, 1955.

Brown, Milton W. *The Story of the Armory Show*. 2nd ed. New York: Abbeville Press, 1988.

Buchholz, Elke Linda. *Women Artists*, trans. Stephen Telfer. Munich, London and New York: Prestel, 2003.

Bucknell, Brad. "On 'Seeing' Salomé," *ELH* 60, no. 2 (1993): 503–26.

Bucur, Maria. "Between the Mother of the Wounded and the Virgin from Jiu. Romanian Women and the Gender of Heroism during the Great War," *Journal of Women's History* 12, no. 2 (2000): 30–56.

Bucur, Maria. *Eugenics and Modernization in Interwar Romania*. Pittsburgh: Pittsburgh University Press, 2002.

Bucur, Maria. "Fallen Women and Necessary Evils: Eugenicist Cultural Representations of and Legal Battles over Prostitution in Interwar Romania," in *"Blood and Homeland." Eugenics and Racial Nationalism in Central and Southeast Europe, 1900-1940*, edited by Marius Turda and Paul Weindling, 335–50. Budapest: Central European University Press, 2007.

Bucur, Maria. *Heroes and Victims: Remembering War in Twentieth-Century Romania*. Bloomington: Indiana University Press, 2009.

Bucur, Maria. "In Praise of Wellborn Mothers. On Eugenics and Gender Roles in Interwar Romania," *East European Politics and Societies* 9, no. 1 (1995): 123–42.

Bucur, Maria. "Remapping the Historiography of Modernization and State-Building in Southeastern Europe through Hygiene, Health and Eugenics," in *Health, Hygiene and Eugenics in Southeastern Europe to 1945*, edited by Marius Turda, Christian Promitzer, and Sevasti Trubeta, 427–46. Budapest: Central European University Press, 2011.

Bucur, Maria. "The Economics of Citizenship: Gender Regimes and Property Rights in Romania in the 20th Century," in *Gender and Citizenship in Historical and Transnational Perspective. Agency, Space, Borders*, edited by Anne R. Eptstein and Rachel G. Fuchs, 143–65. Basingstoke: Palgrave, 2017.

Bucur, Maria, and Mihaela Miroiu, eds. *Patriarhat şi emancipare în istoria gîndirii politice româneşti*. Iaşi: Polirom, 2002.

Butler, Christopher. *Modernism: A Very Short Introduction*. Oxford: Oxford University Press, 2010.

Butler, Cornelia H., and Alexandra Schwartz, eds. *Modern Women: Women Artists at the Museum of Modern Art*. New York: Museum of Modern Art, 2010.

Butler, Judith. *Gender Trouble: Feminism and the Subversion of Identity*. New York: Routledge, 2006.

Callen, Anthea. *Women Artists of the Arts and Crafts Movement, 1870-1914*. New York: Pantheon Books, 1979.

Cavanaugh, Jan. *Out Looking in: Early Modern Polish Art, 1890-1918*. Berkeley: University of California Press, 2000.

Champagne, John. *Aesthetic Modernism and Masculinity in Fascist Italy*. New York: Routledge, 2012.

Chapman, Mary. *Making Noise, Making News: Suffrage Print Culture and U.S. Modernism*. Oxford: Oxford University Press, 2014.

Chave, Anna. *Constantin Brâncuşi: Shifting the Bases of Art*. New Haven: Yale University Press, 1993.

Chodorow, Nancy. *Feminism and Psychoanalytic Theory*. New Haven: Yale University Press, 1989.

Churchill, Suzanne W., and Adam McKible, eds. *Little Magazines & Modernism: New Approaches*. Aldershot: Ashgate, 2007.

Clark, Christopher M. *Sleepwalkers: How Europe Went to War in 1914*. New York: Harper Perennial, 2014.

Clark, Roland. "Die Damen der Legion: Frauen in rumäischen faschistischen Gruppierungen," in *Inszenierte Gegenmacht von rechts: Die "Legion Erzengel Michael" in Rumänien 1918-1938*, edited by Armin Heinen and O. J. Schmitt, 193–216. Munich: Oldenberg Verlag, 2013.

Clark, Suzanne. *Sentimental Modernism: Women Writers and the Revolution of the Word*. Bloomington: Indiana University Press, 1991.

Clark, T. J. *Farewell to an Idea: Episodes from a History of Modernism*. New Haven: Yale University Press, 1999.

Cohler, B. J., and R. M. Galatzer-Levy. "Freud, Anna, and the Problem of Female Sexuality," *Psychoanalytic Inquiry* 28 (2008): 3–26.

Cordón, Luis A. *Freud's World: An Encyclopedia of His Life and Times*. Santa Barbara: Greenwood, 2012.

Crawford, Elizabeth. *The Women's Suffrage Movement: A Reference Guide, 1866-1928*. New York: Routledge, 2001.

Cruikshank, Margaret. *The Gay and Lesbian Liberation Movement*. New York: Routledge, 1992.

Daniel, Lucy Jane. *Gertrude Stein*. London: Reaktion Books, 2009.

de Groot, Cornelis Hofstede. "Judith Leyster," *Jahrbuch der Königlich Preussischen Kunstsammlungen* 14 (1893): 190–98.

de Haan, Francisca, Krasimira Daskalova, and Anna Loutfi, eds. *Biographical Dictionary of Women's Movements and Feminisms in Central, Eastern, and South Eastern Europe. 19th and 20th Centuries*. Budapest: Central European University Press, 2006.

Dearborn, Mary V. *Mistress of Modernism: The Life of Peggy Guggenheim*. Boston: Houghton Mifflin, 2004.

Deepwell, Katy, ed. *Women Artists and Modernism*. Manchester: Manchester University Press, 1998.

Dekoven, Marianne. "Modernism and Gender," in *The Cambridge Companion to Modernism*, edited by Michael Levenson, 174–79. Cambridge: Cambridge University Press, 1993.

Dekoven, Marianne. *Rich and Strange: Gender, History, Modernism*. Princeton: Princeton University Press, 1991.

Dierkes-Thrun, Petra. *Salomé's Modernity: Oscar Wilde and the Aesthetics of Transgression*. Ann Arbor: University of Michigan Press, 2011.

Eagleton, Terry, and Manuel Barbeito, eds. *Modernity, Modernism, Postmodernism: Essays*. Santiago de Compostela: Universidade de Santiago de Compostela, 2000.

Eidelberg, Martin P. *A New Light on Tiffany: Clara Driscoll and the Tiffany Girls*. London: New-York Historical Society, in association with D. Giles Ltd, 2007.

Eley, Geoff. *Forging Democracy the History of the Left in Europe, 1850-2000*. Oxford: Oxford University Press, 2002.

Engler, Barbara. *Personality Theories*. 9th ed. Belmont: Wadsworth, 2014.

English, Daylanne K. *Unnatural Selections. Eugenics in American Modernism and the Harlem Renaissance*. Chapel Hill: University of North Carolina Press, 2004.

Felski, Rita. *The Gender of Modernity*. Cambridge, MA: Harvard University Press, 1995.

Ferguson, Kathy E. "Assemblages of Anarchists: Political Aesthetics in Mother Earth," *The Journal of Modern Periodical Studies* 4, no. 2 (2013): 171–94.

Ferguson, Kathy E. *Emma Goldman: Political Thinking in the Streets*. Lanham: Rowman & Littlefield Publishers, 2011.

Fernihough, Anne. *Freewomen and Supermen: Edwardian Radicals and Literary Modernism*. Oxford: Oxford University Press, 2013.

Fidelis, Malgorzata. *Women, Communism, and Industrialization in Postwar Poland*. New York: Cambridge University Press, 2014.

Finnegan, Margaret Mary. *Selling Suffrage: Consumer Culture & Votes for Women*. New York: Columbia University Press, 1999.

FitzGerald, Michael C. *Making Modernism: Picasso and the Creation of the Market for Twentieth Century Art*. New York: Farrar, Straus and Giroux, 1995.

Foucault, Michel. *The History of Sexuality*. 3 Vols. London: Allen Lane, 1978.

Friedman, Susan Stanford. *Mappings: Feminism and the Cultural Geographies of Encounter*. Princeton: Princeton University Press, 1998.

Fritzsche, Peter. *Germans into Nazis*. Cambridge, MA: Harvard University Press, 1998.

Fritzsche, Peter. *A Nation of Fliers German Aviation and the Popular Imagination*. Cambridge, MA: Harvard University Press, 1992.

Fritzsche, Peter. *Reading Berlin 1900*. Cambridge, MA: Harvard University Press, 1998.

Fussell, Paul. *The Great War and Modern Memory*. 25th anniversary ed. New York: Oxford University Press, 2000.

Gambrell, Alice. *Women Intellectuals, Modernism, and Difference: Transatlantic Culture, 1919-1945*. Cambridge: Cambridge University Press, 1997.

Gere, Charlotte. *Great Women Collectors*. London; New York: P. Wilson; In association with Harry N. Abrams, 1999.

Gilbert, Sandra M., and Susan Gubar, eds. *The Female Imagination and the Modernist Aesthetic*. New York: Gordon and Breach Science Publishers, 1986.

Gilbert, Sandra M., and Susan Gubar. *The Madwoman in the Attic the Woman Writer and the Nineteenth-Century Literary Imagination*. New Haven: Yale University Press, 2000.

Giovacchini, Saverio. *Hollywood Modernism: Film and Politics in the Age of the New Deal*. Philadelphia: Temple University Press, 2001.

Glickman, Lawrence B., ed. *Consumer Society in American History: A Reader*. Ithaca: Cornell University Press, 1999.

Goldman, Emma. *The Social Significance of the Modern Drama*. Boston: Richard G. Badger, 1914.

Goldman, Jonathan L. *Modernism Is the Literature of Celebrity*. Austin: University of Texas Press, 2012.

Goody, Alex. *Modernist Articulations: A Cultural Reading of Djuna Barnes, Mina Loy and Gertrude Stein*. Basingstoke: Palgrave, 2007.

Goscilo, Helena, and Beth Holmgren, eds. *Poles Apart: Women in Modern Polish Culture*. Bloomington: Slavica Publishers, 2006.

Grayzel, Susan R. *Women's Identities at War: Gender, Motherhood, and Politics in Britain and France during the First World War*. Chapel Hill: University of North Carolina Press, 1999.

Griffin, Roger. *Modernism and Fascism: The Sense of a Beginning under Mussolini and Hitler*. Basingstoke: Palgrave Macmillan, 2007.

Guterl, Matthew Pratt. *Josephine Baker and the Rainbow Tribe*. Cambridge: Belknap Press, 2014.

Hanson, Clare. *Eugenics, Literature, and Culture in Post-War Britain*. New York: Routledge, 2013.

Harrison, Elizabeth Jane, and Shirley Peterson, eds. *Unmanning Modernism: Gendered Re-Readings*. Knoxville: University of Tennessee Press, 1997.

Hartsock, Nancy. "Rethinking Modernism: Minority vs. Majority Theories," *Cultural Critique* 7 (1987): 187–206.

Haugen, Einar Ingvald. *Ibsen's Drama: Author to Audience*. Minneapolis: University of Minnesota Press, 1979.

Hau, Michael. *The Cult of Health and Beauty in Germany: A Social History, 1890-1930*. Chicago: The University of Chicago Press, 2003.

Hawthorne, Melanie, and Richard Joseph Golsan, eds. *Gender and Fascism in Modern France*. Hanover: Dartmouth College: University Press of New England, 1997.

Hedrick, Tace. *Mestizo Modernism. Race, Nation, and Identity in Latin American Culture, 1900-1940*. New Brunswick: Rutgers University Press, 2003.

Herf, Jeffrey. *Reactionary Modernism: Technology, Culture, and Politics in Weimar and the Third Reich*. Cambridge: Cambridge University Press, 1984.

Higonnet, Margaret R., Jane Jenson, Sonya Michel, and Margaret Collins Weitz, eds. *Behind the Lines: Gender and the Two World Wars*. New Haven: Yale University Press, 1987.

Hoffman, Frederick J., Charles Allen, and Carolyn F. Ulrich. *The Little Magazine. A History and a Bibliography*. Princeton: Princeton University Press, 1946.

Holmgren, Beth. *Starring Madame Modjeska: On Tour in Poland and America*. Bloomington: Indiana University Press, 2012.

Hubbs, Nadine. *The Queer Composition of America's Sound: Gay Modernists, American Music, and National Identity*. Berkeley: University of California Press, 2004.

Huggins, Mike, and Mike O'Mahony. *The Visual in Sport*. Hoboken: Taylor and Francis, 2013.

Huyssen, Andreas. *After the Great Divide: Modernism, Mass Culture, Postmodernism*. Bloomington: Indiana University Press, 1986.

Izenberg, Gerald N. *Modernism and Masculinity: Mann, Wedekind, Kandinsky through World War I*. Chicago: University of Chicago Press, 2000.

James, David, ed. *The Legacies of Modernism: Historicising Postwar and Contemporary Fiction*. Cambridge: Cambridge University Press, 2012.

Janz, Oliver, and Daniel Schönpflug, eds. *Gender History in a Transnational Perspective: Networks, Biographies, Gender Orders*. New York: Berghahn, 2014.

Jelavich, Peter. *Berlin Cabaret*. Cambridge, MA: Harvard University Press, 1993.

Johnsen, William A., "Madame Bovary: Romanticism, Modernism, and Bourgeois Style," *MLN* 94, no. 4 (1979): 843–50.

Jones, Susan. *Literature, Modernism, and Dance*. Oxford: Oxford University Press, 2013.

Kelly, Michael, ed. *Encyclopedia of Aesthetics*. 4 vols. Oxford: Oxford University Press, 1998.

Kelly-Gadol, Joan. "Did Women Have a Renaissance?," in *Becoming Visible: Women in European History*, edited by Renate Bridenthal and Claudia Koonz, 19–50. Boston: Houghton Mifflin, 1977.

Kline, Wendy. *Building a Better Race: Gender, Sexuality, and Eugenics from the Turn of the Century to the Baby Boom*. Berkeley: University of California Press, 2005.

Knöfel, Ulrike. "The Legacy of Modernism: Celebrating 90 Years of Bauhaus," *Spiegel International*, February 27, 2009, at http://www.spiegel.de/international/zeitgeist/the-legacy-of-modernism-celebrating-90-years-of-bauhaus-a-610283.html (accessed March 10, 2015).

Kolocotroni, Vassiliki, Jane Goldman, and Olga Taxidou, eds. *Modernism: An Anthology of Sources and Documents*. Chicago: University of Chicago Press, 1998.

Kosta, Barbara. *Willing Seduction: The Blue Angel, Marlene Dietrich, and Mass Culture*. New York: Berghahn Books, 2009.

Kuhn, Walt. *The Story of the Armory Show*. New York: Self-published, 1938.

Kushner, Marilyn S., Kimberly Orcutt, and Casey Nelson Blake. *The Armory Show at 100: Modernism and Revolution*. New York: New York Historical Society, 2013.

Laqueur, Thomas Walter. *Making Sex: Body and Gender from the Greeks to Freud*. Cambridge, MA: Harvard University Press, 1990.

Leighten, Patricia. "The White Peril and *L'Art nègre*: Picasso, Primitivism, and Anticolonialism," *The Art Bulletin* 72, no. 4 (1990): 609–30.

Lemke, Sieglinde. *Primitivist Modernism: Black Culture and the Origins of Transatlantic Modernism*. Oxford: Oxford University Press, 1998.

Levenback, Karen L. *Virginia Woolf and the Great War*. Syracuse: Syracuse University Press, 1999.

Lewis, Pericles, ed. *The Cambridge Companion to European Modernism*. Cambridge Companions to Topics. Cambridge: Cambridge University Press, 2011.

Lines, Lisa Margaret. *Milicianas: Women in Combat in the Spanish Civil War*. Lanham: Lexington Books, 2012.

Lowe, Sarah M. *Frida Kahlo*. New York: Universe Publishing, 1991.

Lunn, Eugene. *Marxism and Modernism: An Historical Study of Lukács, Brecht, Benjamin, and Adorno*. Berkeley: University of California Press, 1982.

Macleod, Dianne Sachko. *Enchanted Lives, Enchanted Objects: American Women Collectors and the Making of Culture, 1800-1940*. Berkeley: University of California Press, 2008.

MacPhee, Josh, and Erik Ruin, eds. *Realizing the Impossible. Art Against Authority*. Oakland: AK Press, 2007.

Marcu, George, ed. *Dicţionarul personalităţilor feminine din România*. Bucharest: Editura Meronia, 2009.

Marek, Jayne E. *Women Editing Modernism: "Little" Magazines & Literary History*. Lexington: University Press of Kentucky, 1995.

Martin, Carol, ed. *A Sourcebook of Feminist Theatre and Performance: On and beyond the Stage*. New York: Routledge, 1996.

Mazumdar, Sucheta, Vasant Kaiwar, and Thierry Labica, eds. *From Orientalism to Postcolonialism: Asia-Europe and the Lineages of Difference*. London: Routledge, 2011.

McCabe, Susan. *Cinematic Modernism Modernist Poetry and Film*. Cambridge: Cambridge University Press, 2009.

McFarlane, James Walter, ed. *The Cambridge Companion to Ibsen*. Cambridge: Cambridge University Press, 1994.

Meecham, Pam. *Modern Art: A Critical Introduction*. 2nd ed. London: Routledge, 2005.

Mews, Siegfried, ed. *A Bertolt Brecht Reference Companion*. Westport: Greenwood Press, 1997.

Micale, Mark S., ed. *The Mind of Modernism: Medicine, Psychology, and the Cultural Arts in Europe and America, 1880-1940*. Stanford: Stanford University Press, 2004.

Miller, Louise. *A Fine Brother: The Life of Captain Flora Sandes*. Richmond, UK: Alma Books, 2014.

Miller, Sanda. "Brâncuși's 'Column of the Infinite'," *The Burlington Magazine* 122, no. 928 (1980): 470–80.

Minden, Michael, and Holger Bachmann. *Fritz Lang's "Metropolis": Cinematic Views of Technology and Fear*. Columbia, SC; Woodbridge: Camden House; Boydell & Brewer, 2002.

Mitchell, Juliet, and Sangay K Mishra. *Psychoanalysis and Feminism: A Radical Reassessment of Freudian Psychoanalysis*, 2d rev. ed. New York: Basic Books, 2000.

Mosse, George L. *The Image of Man: The Creation of Modern Masculinity*. New York: Oxford University Press, 1996.

Nochlin, Linda. "Why Have There Been No Great Women Artists?," in *Women, Art and Power and Other Essays*, 147–58. New York: Westview Press, 1988.

Nolan, Elizabeth, and Janet Beer, eds. *Kate Chopin's The Awakening: A Sourcebook*. London: Routledge, 2004.

Noun, Louise. *Abastenia St. Leger Eberle, Sculptor (1878-1942)*. Des Moines: Des Moines Art Center, 1980.

Noun, Louise. *Three Berlin artists of the Weimar Era: Hannah Höch, Käth e Kollwitz, Jeanne Mammen*. Des Moines: Des Moines Art Center, 1994.

Oosterhuis, Harry. "Sexual Modernity in the Works of Richard von Krafft-Ebing and Albert Moll," *Medical History* 56, no. 2 (2012): 133–55.

Oosterhuis, Harry. *Stepchildren of Nature: Krafft-Ebing, Psychiatry, and the Making of Sexual Identity*. Chicago: University of Chicago Press, 2000.

Passmore, Kevin, ed. *Women, Gender, and Fascism in Europe, 1919-45*. New Brunswick: Manchester University Press, 2003.

Pateman, Carole. *The Sexual Contract*. Stanford: Stanford University Press, 1988.

Peel, Robert A., and Galton Institute, eds. *Marie Stopes, Eugenics and the English Birth Control Movement*. London: Galton Institute, 1997.

Peppis, Paul. *Sciences of Modernism: Ethnography, Sexology, and Psychology*. New York: Cambridge University Press, 2014.

Perrie, Maureen, ed. *The Cambridge History of Russia*. Cambridger: Cambridge University Press, 2006.

Perry, Gillian, ed. *Gender and Art*. New Haven: Yale University Press, 1999.

Petro, Patrice. *Joyless Streets: Women and Melodramatic Representation in Weimar Germany*. Princeton: Princeton University Press, 1989.

Pevsner, Nikolaus. *Academies of Art. Past and Present*. London: Cambridge University Press, 1940.

Phillips, Duncan. *The Eye of Duncan Phillips: A Collection in the Making*. Washington, DC: Phillips Collection in association with Yale University New Haven, 1999.

Piland, Sherry. *Women Artists: An Historical, Contemporary, and Feminist Bibliography*. 2nd ed. Metuchen: Scarecrow Press, 1994.

Pollock, Griselda. *Avant-Garde Gambits, 1888-1893: Gender and the Color of Art History*. New York: Thames and Hudson, 1993.

Pollock, Griselda. *Vision and Difference: Femininity, Feminism, and Histories of Art*. London: Routledge, 1988.

Pollock, Griselda. "Women, Art, and Art History: Gender and Feminist Analyses," in *Oxford Bibliographies*. Oxford: Oxford University Press, at http://www.oxfordbibliographies.com/view/document/obo-9780199920105/obo-9780199920105-0034.xml.

Porter, Laurence M., ed. *A Gustave Flaubert Encyclopedia*. Westport: Greenwood Press, 2001.

Rachamimov, Alon. "The Disruptive Comforts of Drag: (Trans)Gender Performances among Prisoners of War in Russia, 1914–1920," *The American Historical Review* 111, no. 2 (2006): 362–82.

Rado, Lisa, ed. *Modernism, Gender, and Culture: A Cultural Studies Approach*. New York: Garland, 1997.

Rainey, Lawrence S., ed. *Modernism: An Anthology*. Malden: Blackwell, 2005.

Ramanathan, Geetha. *Locating Gender in Modernism: The Outsider Female*. New York: Routledge, 2012.

Roberts, Andrew Lawrence. *From Good King Wenceslas to the Good Soldier Švejk a Dictionary of Czech Popular Culture*. Budapest: Central European University Press, 2005.

Rolland, Denis. *La Grève Des Tranchées: Les Mutineries de 1917*. Paris: Imago, 2005.

Roworth, Wendy Wassying, ed. *Angelica Kauffman. A Continental Artist in Georgian England*. London: Reaktion Books, 1992.

Rubin, William, Helene Seckel, and Judith Cousins. *Les Demoiselles d'Avignon*. New York: The Museum of Modern Art, 1995.

Rupp, Leila J. *Worlds of Women: The Making of an International Women's Movement*. Princeton: Princeton University Press, 1997.

Rutsky, R. L. "The Mediation of Technology and Gender: Metropolis, Nazism, Modernism," *New German Critique* 60 (1993): 3–32.

Sartori, Eva Martin, and Dorothy Wynne Zimmerman, eds. *French Women Writers: A Bio-Bibliographical Source Book*. New York: Greenwood Press, 1991.

Scandura, Jani, and Michael Thurston, eds. *Modernism, Inc.: Body, Memory, Capital*. New York: New York University Press, 2001.

Schmidt, Georg, ed. *Sophie Taeuber-Arp*. Basel: Holbein Verlag, 1948.

Schorske, Carl E. *Fin-de-Siècle Vienna: Politics and Culture.* 1st Vintage Book ed. New York: Vintage Books, 1981.

Schwartz, Agata. *Gender and Modernity in Central Europe: The Austro-Hungarian Monarchy and Its Legacy.* Ottawa: University of Ottawa Press, 2010.

Scott, Bonnie Kime, ed. *Gender in Modernism: New Geographies, Complex Intersections.* Urbana: University of Illinois Press, 2007.

Scott, Bonnie Kime, and Mary Lynn Broe, eds. *The Gender of Modernism: A Critical Anthology.* Bloomington: Indiana University Press, 1990.

Scott, Joan W. "Gender: A Useful Category of Historical Analysis," *The American Historical Review* 91, no. 5 (1986): 1053–75.

Scott, William B., and Peter M Rutkoff. *New York Modern: The Arts and the City.* Baltimore: Johns Hopkins University Press, 1999.

Segel, Harold B. *Turn-of-the-Century Cabaret: Paris, Barcelona, Berlin, Munich, Vienna, Cracow, Moscow, St. Petersburg, Zurich.* New York: Columbia University Press, 1987.

Severi, Rita. "Oscar Wilde, La Femme Fatale and the Salomé Myth," in *Proceedings of the Xth Congress of the International Comparative Literature Association,* edited by Anna Balakian and James Wilhelm, 458–63. New York: Garland, 1985.

Shanes, Eric. *Constantin Brâncuşi.* New York: Abbeville Press, 1989.

Shaughnessy, Nicola, and British Council. *Gertrude Stein.* Tavistock: Northcote/British Council, 2007.

Sheffield, Suzanne Le-May. *Women and Science: Social Impact and Interaction.* New Brunswick: Rutgers University Press, 2006.

Shepherd, Simon. *Drama/Theatre/Performance.* London: Routledge, 2004.

Sherman, Daniel J. *The Construction of Memory in Interwar France.* Chicago: University of Chicago Press, 1999.

Shiach, Morag, ed. *The Cambridge Companion to the Modernist Novel.* Cambridge: Cambridge University Press, 2007.

Shiraev, Eric. *A History of Psychology: A Global Perspective.* Thousand Oaks: SAGE, 2011.

Shircliff, Jennifer Pfeifer, "Women of the 1913 Armory Show: Their Contributions to the Development of American Modern Art," PhD diss., University of Louisville, Louisville, 2014.

Showalter, Elaine. *Sexual Anarchy: Gender and Culture at the Fin de Siècle.* London: Virago, 1992.

Shulman, Alix Kates. *To the Barricades the Anarchist Life of Emma Goldman.* New York: Open Road Integrated Media, 2011.

Smith, Angela K. *The Second Battlefield: Women, Modernism and the First World War.* Manchester: Manchester University Press, 2000.

Smith, Kimberly A. *Between Ruin and Renewal: Egon Schiele's Landscapes.* New Haven: Yale University Press, 2004.

Smith, Leonard V. *The Embattled Self: French Soldiers' Testimony of the Great War.* Ithaca: Cornell University Press, 2007.

Solomon, Alisa. *Re-Dressing the Canon: Essays on Theater and Gender.* London: Routledge, 1997.

Sonn, Richard David. *Sex, Violence, and the Avant-Garde: Anarchism in Interwar France.* University Park: Pennsylvania State University Press, 2010.

Spackman, Barbara. *Fascist Virilities: Rhetoric, Ideology, and Social Fantasy in Italy.* Minneapolis: University of Minnesota Press, 1996.

Stansell, Christine. *Feminist Promise*. New York: Random House, 2011.

Staples, Shelley, "'The Part Played By Women': The Gender of Modernism at the Armory Show," at http://xroads.virginia.edu/~museum/armory/gender.html (created May 2001).

Stepan, Nancy. *The Hour of Eugenics: Race, Gender, and Nation in Latin America*. Ithaca: Cornell University Press, 1991.

Stephenson, Andrew. "'New Ways of Modern Bohemia': Edward Burra in London, Paris, Marseilles and Harlem," *Tate Papers* 19 (2013), at http://www.tate.org.uk/research/publications/tate-papers/19/new-ways-of-modern-bohemia-edward-burra-in-london-paris-marseilles-and-harlem (accessed October 19, 2016).

Stockard, Jean, and Miriam M. Johnson. *Sex and Gender in Society*. 2nd ed. Englewood Cliffs: Prentice Hall, 1992.

Stoff, Laurie. *They Fought for the Motherland: Russia's Women Soldiers in World War I* and *the Revolution*. Lawrence: University Press of Kansas, 2006.

Suleiman, Susan Rubin. *Subversive Intent: Gender, Politics, and the Avant-Garde*. Cambridge, MA: Harvard University Press, 2012.

Sweeney, Carole. *From Fetish to Subject: Race, Modernism, and Primitivism, 1919-1935*. Westport: Praeger Publishers, 2004.

Swiencicki, Mark A. "Consuming Brotherhood. Men's Culture, Style and Recreation as Consumer Culture, 1880-1930," in *Consumer Society in American History. A Reader*, edited by Lawrence B. Glickman, 207–40. Ithaca: Cornell University Press, 1999.

Thébaud, Françoise. *A History of Women in the West*. 5 vols. Cambridge: Belknap Press, 1998.

Theweleit, Klaus. *Male Fantasies*. Minneapolis: University of Minnesota Press, 1987.

Thomson, Peter, and Glendyr Sacks, eds. *The Cambridge Companion to Brecht*. 2nd ed. Cambridge: Cambridge University Press, 2006.

Tickner, Lisa. *The Spectacle of Women: Imagery of the Suffrage Campaign, 1907-14*. Chicago: University of Chicago Press, 1988.

Toepfer, Karl Eric. *Empire of Ecstasy: Nudity and Movement in German Body Culture, 1910-1935*. Berkeley: University of California Press, 1997.

Toulalan, Sarah, and Kate Fisher, eds. *The Routledge History of Sex and the Body: 1500 to the Present*. Abingdon and New York: Routledge, 2013.

Townsend, Julie. "Un-Fixing Baker. Against a Criticism of Stasis," *Modernist Cultures* 9, no. 1 (2014): 62–70.

Turda, Marius. *Modernism and Eugenics*. Basingstoke: Palgrave, 2010.

Turda, Marius, and Paul Weindling, eds. *"Blood and Homeland": Eugenics and Racial Nationalism in Central and Southeast Europe, 1900-1940*. Budapest: Central European University Press, 2007.

Veder, Robin. "Seeing Your Way to Health: The Visual Pedagogy of Bess Mensendieck's Physical Culture System," *International Journal of the History of Sport* 28, nos. 8–9 (2011): 1336–52.

Vujnović, Marina. "Forging the Bubikopf Nation: A Feminist Political-Economic Analysis of *Ženski List*, Interwar Croatia's Women's magazine, for the Construction of an Alternative Vision of Modernity." PhD diss., University of Iowa, Iowa City, 2009.

Walz, Robin. *Modernism*, 2nd ed. Abingdon: Routledge, 2013.

Wardle, Marian, ed. *American Women Modernists. The Legacy of Robert Henri, 1910-1945*. Provo: Brigham Young University Museum of Art; New Brunswick: Rutgers University Press, 2005.

Warlick, M. E. *Max Ernst and Alchemy: A Magician in Search of Myth*. Austin: University of Texas Press, 2001.

Weir, Robert E. *Workers in America: A Historical Encyclopedia*. Santa Barbara: ABC-CLIO, 2013.

Weisberg, Gabriel P., Jane R. Becker, Sterling and Francine Clark Art Institute, Dahesh Museum, and Dixon Gallery and Gardens, eds. *Overcoming All Obstacles: The Women of the Académie Julian*. New York and New Brunswick: Dahesh Museum; Rutgers University Press, 1999.

Weitz, Eric D. *Weimar Germany: Promise and Tragedy*. Princeton: Princeton University Press, 2007.

Will, Barbara. *Gertrude Stein, Modernism, and the Problem of "Genius."* Edinburgh: Edinburgh University Press, 2000.

Williams, John A. *"The Blue Angel (Der Blaue Engel)* by Josef von Sternberg," *Modernism/modernity* 20, no. 4 (2013): 801–04.

Williams, Raymond. *The Politics of Modernism: Against the New Conformists*. New York: Verso, 1989.

Wingfield, Nancy M., and Maria Bucur, eds. *Gender and War in Twentieth-Century Eastern Europe*. Bloomington: Indiana University Press, 2006.

Wolfe, Jesse. *Bloomsbury, Modernism, and the Reinvention of Intimacy*. Cambridge: Cambridge University Press, 2011.

Wood, Elizabeth A. *The Baba and the Comrade: Gender and Politics in Revolutionary Russia*. Bloomington: Indiana University Press, 1997.

Wood, Nathaniel D. *Becoming Metropolitan: Urban Selfhood and the Making of Modern Cracow*. DeKalb: Northern Illinois University Press, 2010.

Young, Julian. *Friedrich Nietzsche: A Philosophical Biography*. Cambridge: Cambridge University Press, 2010.

Zox-Weaver, Annalisa. *Women Modernists and Fascism: Female Modernists and the Allure of the Dictator*. Cambridge: Cambridge University Press, 2011.

Index

9 781350 026254